THE POWER OF SOCIAL SKILLS IN CHARACTER DEVELOPMENT

HELPING DIVERSE LEARNERS SUCCEED

Jennifer L. Scully

DUDE PUBLISHING
A Division of
National Professional Resources, Inc.
Port Chester, New York

Scully, Jennifer L.
    The power of social skills in character
development: helping diverse learners succeed.
Jennifer L. Scully—1st ed.
    p. cm.
    Includes bibliographical references.
    ISBN: 1-887943-42-0
1. Character. 2. Social skills in children

I. Title.

LC268.S38 2000   370.114
                                   QBI00-384

Cover design and
book design by
Faith E. Deegan
Faith Design, Mamaroneck, New York

Dude Publishing
A division of National Professional Resources, Inc.
25 South Regent Street
Port Chester, New York 10573
Toll free: (800) 453–7461
Phone: (914) 937–8879

Visit our Web site: www.nprinc.com

Printed in the United States of America

ISBN 1-887943-42-0

To Jessica, Katie, Lauren, Jason, Daniel, Cassandra, Thomas, and Mary Frances.

I see hopes and dreams in your eyes...
chase after them and succeed!

CONTENTS

UNIT III: RELATIONSHIPS

UNIT IV: CRITICISM AND ATTITUDES

UNIT V: STRESS MANAGEMENT

UNIT VI: CONFLICT RESOLUTION AND PROBLEM SOLVING

ACKNOWLEDGMENTS

SPECIAL THANKS TO:

My parents, Patricia and Paul, for teaching me right from wrong and showing me a lifetime of love and support.

All of my students: You are truly special people and this book is the result of all of your hard work and good character. Thanks for making every moment a teaching moment.

Dr. Roger Fazzone, Maplebrook School, and the Board of Trustees for allowing me the time to undertake this project and for offering their support.

Ms. Priscilla Buckley for your invaluable advice, as well as my brother Michael and Donna Konkolics for taking the time to proofread.

Andrea Cerone of the NPR staff for her editorial assistance.

Most importantly, Tina Coddington for your friendship, patience and understanding. I cannot thank you enough for the years of happiness and laughter you have helped to create.

INTRODUCTION

As an experienced teacher, I have come to appreciate the importance of character education and social skills training for adolescents. I became especially aware of this during my years of teaching students with learning differences. These students, in particular, needed help in coping with a variety of issues in their lives, such as developing friendships, showing self-control, communicating properly, solving problems, making moral judgments, and the like. While the lessons in this book were developed specifically for students with learning differences, the program can be used for other students as well. We can easily cite many circumstances in which home and community environments have left students ill equipped to deal with social interactions with their peers, teachers, and adults outside the school.

We all know that, for success in life, students must demonstrate not only academic ability but also social competence. This assertion has found support in countless studies. Research by Warger and Rutherford (1993), for example, emphasizes the importance of peer and teacher acceptance. For students to receive the maximum benefit from their education, this acceptance must accompany learning. Along with other factors, acceptance provides a stable environment in which to learn.

While many conditions influence the development of social competence, there are clearly advantages to a *structured* social skills program. A structured program, by its very nature, covers a spectrum of needed social skills. It helps students improve self-esteem, student/teacher relationships, peer relationships, and the school climate as a whole.

The lessons in this book were designed to help teachers, parents, and other professionals guide and teach specific social skills. The program's major objectives are to help students build self-esteem, respect for themselves and others, responsibility for their actions, and good character. By character, we mean "operative values" as well as "knowing the good, desiring the good, and doing the good" (Lickona 1991). It is important to tap the values that parents teach their children and enhance those values by helping students realize that it is in their nature to respond to situations in a morally responsible way. Furthermore, we teachers must model moral behavior. When we show respect and act as responsible people, both in and out of the classroom, we are speaking volumes to our students.

Students using these lessons will show marked improvement in social awareness. I have seen the results with my own students, and I am confident that other professionals who adapt and apply the lessons will experience similar results—and similar satisfaction from seeing their students mature socially. These are skills that students will use not only in their school years, but also throughout their lives.

This resource is divided into 80 lessons within seven units. Teachers will find detailed social skill lessons, reproducible activities, and homework assignments included in each lesson. The lessons are presented in a uniform format and follow a structured learning approach to both social skills and character education. The lessons in this resource have been classroom-tested for effectiveness.

Carter and Sugai (1989) have suggested six strategies to assist in teaching social skills: modeling, strategic placement, correspondence training, rehearsal and practice, positive reinforcement, and prompting and coaching. These are all effective tools to ensure successful social skills training, and I have incorporated elements of this model into the lessons.

Clearly, we need to address the growing problem of lack of social skills and character education in our adolescents. This program will help them cope with the issues in their lives, such as developing friendships, showing self-control, communicating properly, solving problems, relying on their moral judgment, etc.

Every classroom is a haven for learning and every teacher is a protector of his or her students' learning. We have the ability to shape lives and foster hope in our students. Our expectation is that they will be able to lead successful, happy, and socially productive lives. We need to work together and take on the responsibility of teaching with patience, caring, respect, and the fervor we had when we first entered the teaching profession.

Rekindle the spark of education, and you will see how the fire of learning spreads. Challenge yourselves to challenge your students. Do not let your students give up, not when help is right around the corner.

"Success is not the result of spontaneous combustion.
You must set yourself on fire."
- Reggie Leach -

The Power of Social Skills in Character Development | Introduction

TEACHER NOTES

The following program is designed to present important skills and concepts of social interaction to students who experience difficulty in social situations. The social skills presented in the program are crucial to building character and improving social success.

Each lesson plan states an objective for the lesson, then presents a class or discussion activity, a group or individual activity (with reproducible exercises), and a suggested homework assignment based on an experiential learning model. With experiential learning, the student is given the opportunity to reflect on both positive and negative personal experiences, then formulate possible changes to improve performance. Students are allowed to practice a particular solution and reevaluate their success. This is an important model to use because it allows each student to become an integral part of his/her intervention as well as an active participant in his/her success.

The program provides opportunities for students to practice reflective thinking as well as interpersonal skills. The following activities support this objective:

Class Discussions:

> Discussions provide a forum in which students can offer suggestions for handling social interactions. Peer feedback is beneficial as students learn to trust each other, "open themselves up," and share their insights.

Role-Playing:

> The role-plays are personal situations based on the real-life experiences of students. Their authenticity allows students to connect with a particular situation and demonstrate their ability with a certain skill. Teachers should observe role-playing and offer corrective comments when necessary.

Homework:

> The homework assignments are designed as journals. The assignments encourage students to reflect on their

own life experiences and apply the skill learned for the day. This provides an opportunity to think about how situations could be handled differently.

Value Journal:

The value journal is used most effectively as a private interaction between the teacher and student. A journal is a way the students can reflect on their own moral judgment and take personal responsibility for acting in accordance with their own value base.

Be aware that parents in some communities have objected to the use of the word *values* in instructional contexts. As used in this program, *values* refers to character traits or virtues that are deeply admired and respected in virtually all societies—honesty, responsibility, commitment, kindness, citizenship, courage, and the like. If there is sensitivity in your community, you may need to clarify how you are using the term and invite parents to participate in identifying admirable character traits they would like the schools to emphasize.

You will find that your students learn more about themselves—and you may be shocked to discover how much you learn about yourself—while using the program. Believe in your students and realize how special these people are; after all, they are our future!

UNIT I

SELF-AWARENESS

In this unit, students will recognize and explore the things that are important to them, as well as character traits and principles they respect and value. At the same time, they will work toward understanding their social deficits and use this understanding as a foundation for personal growth. (Students must understand their needs before they can put a self-improvement plan into motion.) Students will grasp how vital self-worth is to building character and for becoming more socially aware. Each student will develop his/her value base and use this value base as a guide for judging and monitoring behavior.

LESSON 1: SELF-ESTEEM
UNIT: SELF-AWARENESS

OBJECTIVE: To explore self-esteem, its meaning to the student and how self-esteem can help in the discovery of assets and strengths.

ACTIVITY: Hand out Self-Esteem Questionnaire on the next page and ask students to complete the questionnaire. Once collected, review and put aside until the last day of the term. This will be used as a comparative measure of each student's view of him/herself.

Group Activity:

1. Define *self-esteem* as having confidence in and satisfaction with yourself. As a class, determine the best working definition.

2. Discuss what self-esteem means to you. Brainstorm characteristics of someone who has healthy self-esteem. Discuss why it is important.

HOMEWORK: *Journal topic:* Write about how you see yourself. Be sure to show an honest expression of yourself.

SELF-ESTEEM

QUESTIONNAIRE

KEY: A = agree · D = disagree · U = undecided

Answer the following questions using one of the letters above.

_____ 1. I feel like I make a lot of mistakes.

_____ 2. I try to impress other people often.

_____ 3. It's no use trying when I know I'll fail.

_____ 4. I feel people talk about me behind my back.

_____ 5. I put myself down.

_____ 6. I don't express my opinion because people won't listen.

_____ 7. I compare myself to others.

_____ 8. I usually think the worst: it's better to be prepared.

_____ 9. I wonder why people are nice to me.

_____ 10. I feel uncomfortable when people give me compliments.

_____ 11. I often feel embarrassed.

_____ 12. I am jealous of others.

_____ 13. I think about what others have and I don't.

_____ 14. I wonder what people think of me.

_____ 15. I apologize for things so others won't be mad at me.

Adapted from Doody & Dick - see bibliography

LESSON 2: VALUES ASSESSMENT
UNIT: SELF-AWARENESS

OBJECTIVE: To define and establish each student's core values and develop value journals. Students will write in their value journals each week as a reflective tool.

Group Activity:

1. Define *values* as those personality traits and principles that we respect and admire and consider important in life.

2. As a class, brainstorm a list of the different values (e.g., respect, responsibility, honesty, faith, love, etc.).

3. Define and discuss each value on the list to be sure of complete understanding.

4. As a class, vote on the top five values for the class to follow.

ACTIVITY: *Value Journal:* Once the values are defined, each student chooses the four values that are the most important to him/her. These should be the values that the student not only believes in, but also lives his or her life by. Students should list their four personal values, using different colored markers, in the front cover of a spiral notebook. At the end of each week, the students will reflect on the activity of the week and write about how they showed their core values that week—or how they were tempted not to show them. Encourage the students to discuss what should have been done to avoid the temptation not to live by their personal values.

HOMEWORK: On the first page of the value journal, answer the question: What does it mean to be a good person?

Teacher tip:
Begin your own value journal.
We cannot help the students
understand their values until
we understand what we value.

LESSON 3: SELF-ADVERTISEMENTS
UNIT: SELF-AWARENESS

OBJECTIVE: To explore self-esteem as it pertains to students' views of themselves and of their strengths and weaknesses.

Group Activity:

1. Review the class definition of self-esteem and lists of characteristics of someone with healthy self-esteem (e.g., accepts responsibility, is honest, smiles, is active, etc.).

2. On a separate sheet of paper, students list their strengths and special skills. (They should try for at least ten.) They may want to complete the sentence, "I am good at…"

3. With the above list, help students come up with a slogan for themselves. You may want to provide examples: "I'm on your side because…," "You're in good hands with…," etc.

ACTIVITY: Distribute sheets of colored poster board. Students write their slogans in large letters at the top. They may choose to either draw or cut out pictures representing the items on their lists of strengths and special skills. Remind them that these are posters that advertise themselves and should display the reasons that other people are privileged to know them. Encourage students to include their values.

HOMEWORK: Describe your special characteristics and why you are an important person. Why are you someone we should like to get to know better?

LESSON 4: SELF-CONCEPT: GENUINE AND REALISTIC?

UNIT: SELF-AWARENESS

OBJECTIVE: To develop a realistic view of oneself, and to recognize those characteristics that are idealistic.

Group Activity:

1. Define *self-concept* as the mental image we have of ourselves. Define *realistic* and *idealistic*:

   • *Realistic:* The things you believe about yourself, "the *true* you."

   • *Idealistic:* The things you would like to be true of yourself, "the *perfect* you."

2. Brainstorm and define adjectives that describe someone with a healthy self-concept, using the characteristic worksheet on the next page.

3. Allow students to add other adjectives they feel should be included.

ACTIVITY: Using the characteristic worksheet, place an **X** next to the adjectives that describe the realistic you. (What you know to be true of you.) Next, circle the adjectives that describe the ideal you. (What you would like to be true of you.) Choose one circled adjective and write it on the line at the bottom of the worksheet. This represents what you would like to change about yourself.

HOMEWORK: List things you can do today to change an idealistic characteristic into a realistic one.

Adapted from Doody and Dick (1980)

CHARACTERISTIC WORKSHEET

GENERAL TRAITS:

nice   patient   helpful   funny

determined   wise   creative   thoughtful

polite   honest   trustworthy   friendly

hardworking   imaginative   confident   athletic

enthusiastic   caring   citizenship   attractive

intelligent   encouraging   positive   considerate

Add any other characteristics that you feel are necessary for a healthy self-concept.

I would like to be more _____.

A PLAN TO CHANGE

I can be more _____ if I :

LESSON 5: CHARACTERISTICS I VALUE
UNIT: SELF-AWARENESS

OBJECTIVE: To further develop values and determine how these values will enhance character development and assist in good judgment.

Group Activity:

1. Review class list of core values.

2. Discuss concepts of right and wrong. Offer hypothetical questions such as, "Is it right or wrong to drive over the speed limit when you are late for a meeting?" (Answers will vary.)

3. Ask students what they believe in as well as why those beliefs are important to them.

ACTIVITY: Distribute the survey on the next page and allow students to complete independently. When completed, discuss answers.

HOMEWORK: Which of the beliefs from your value survey are the most important to you and why? Write your response in your value journal.

VALUE SURVEY -

WHAT CHARACTER TRAITS AND PRINCIPLES DO I VALUE?

1. If you saw someone in a disabled car on the highway, would you stop to help?

2. What role does your family play in your life?

3. How do you disagree with your parents?

4. If you were hungry and had no income, would you steal food to feed yourself? What if you had a family?

5. When is it okay to break a rule or law?

6. Is religion a part of your life? If so, how?

7. Do you believe that people are generally good or generally bad? Why?

8. Do you help in your community? If so, how?

9. Would you make jokes about someone's appearance if everyone else did?

10. Would you turn in your best friend for shoplifting?

SELF-AWARENESS

QUOTATIONS OF THE WEEK:

"You must begin to think of yourself as becoming the person you want to be."
- David Viscott -

"We all feel more beautiful when we are loved. And when you have self-love, you are always beautiful."
- Alice Walker -

"Character is destiny."
- Heraclitus -

"The price of greatness is responsibility."
- Winston Churchill -

"The outside mask is not the same as the inside experience."
- Virginia Satir -

"Man's self-concept is enhanced when he takes responsibility for himself."
- William C. Schultz -

Teacher tip:

Pin one of the quotations above to a bulletin board and ask students to reflect on what is said, apply it to their thinking, and explain if they agree with it. You may have them write about it in their value journals.

COMMUNICATION SKILLS

The communication skills unit will help students recognize and use appropriate body language, including nonverbal messages. They will understand that by expressing their feelings using "I" statements, they are taking responsibility and showing courtesy and respect. Students will realize how easy it is to send mixed messages and how difficult it is to listen. In addition, students will learn how to interrupt appropriately, engage in conversations, and avoid communication blocks. They will discover not only that it takes a great deal of effort to communicate properly, but also that cooperation and respect are necessary elements for successful communication.

LESSON 6: COMMUNICATION BASICS
UNIT: COMMUNICATION SKILLS

OBJECTIVE: To achieve a greater awareness of the basic need for communication.

Group Activity:

1. As a class, create a working definition of *communication* and discuss what it means to communicate.

2. Brainstorm examples of ways to communicate. If necessary, explain and/or define each way to ensure complete understanding.

ACTIVITY: Divide the class into small groups of no more than four students each. Distribute poster board and magazines for each group. Create collages illustrating ways to communicate. Be sure each poster gives an explanation of the method of communication.

HOMEWORK: What is hard about communicating with others, and why is it difficult for you?

LESSON 7: BODY LANGUAGE & NONVERBAL MESSAGES
UNIT: COMMUNICATION SKILLS

OBJECTIVE: To read and understand messages sent with body language and with subtle social cues, and to develop habits of using body language that is appropriate to the message being sent.

Group Activity:

1. Define body language and nonverbal messages.

2. Brainstorm examples of nonverbal messages (e.g., hand gestures, smiling, shrugging shoulders, etc.).

3. Discuss how people's moods are shown through body language and give examples.

ACTIVITY: Role-play both appropriate and inappropriate body language using the situations on the next page. Ask for class volunteers. When finished, discuss why some are acceptable and some are not.

HOMEWORK: "Say What?" activity found on page 15.

MESSAGE CENTER

DIRECTIONS: Use the following role-play situations to practice recognizing and using appropriate body language. What are the messages each person is sending?

1. Your friend comes into the room with her head lowered and shoulders slumped. When you ask what is wrong, she snaps, "Nothing!"

2. Your teacher gets up from her desk, stands before the class and folds her arms. She does not say a word.

3. A classmate bursts into the room, out of breath and sweating, and falls in a heap into his chair.

4. You are telling a story about your summer vacation and one person in the group yawns, stretches and slouches in the chair.

5. You walk up to a group of your friends and they stop talking. You notice that one girl rolls her eyes.

6. After telling your sister not to take your favorite sweater, you notice it missing from your closet. You ask her if she has seen it. She looks around the room, hesitates and says, "Ummm....no, I haven't."

7. You are at a party and your host spills a tray of drinks in your lap. His face turns red. He clears his voice and smiles awkwardly.

8. You sit in the dentist's chair and she comes into the room with a big smile and tells you, "This won't hurt a bit."

"SAY WHAT?"

Name_____ Date_____

DIRECTIONS: Read each character's body language and fill in the ballons wih the appropriate dialogue.

LESSON 8: EFFECTIVE COMMUNICATION
UNIT: COMMUNICATION SKILLS

OBJECTIVE: To send and receive messages in an understandable manner while paying attention to body language.

Group Activity:

1. Define *effective communication* as communication that is understandable and accomplishes what we set out to do. (The person receiving the message understands the message.)

2. Discuss how a person can be speaking and at the same time pay attention to nonverbal messages. Give examples if necessary (e.g., eye contact, using a clear voice, etc.).

3. List and discuss helpful skill hints for sending messages effectively:

   • Make eye contact.

   • Use simple language.

   • Make nonverbal messages match what you are saying.

   • Know what you want to say BEFORE you say it.

ACTIVITY: In partners, students first try to communicate without speaking. Encourage students to use as much body language as possible. Discuss results when finished. Emphasize and compare this activity with giving someone wrong information. How important is effective communication?

HOMEWORK: What does your body language say to others? How important is it to communicate effectively?

LESSON 9: "I" STATEMENTS
UNIT: COMMUNICATION SKILLS

OBJECTIVE: To learn to take responsibility for how we feel, without offending others.

Group Activity:

1. Define *"I" statements*. Example: By using the pronoun "I" when we express something, we "own" and take responsibility for our feelings.

2. Discuss how "I" statements have positive effects on listeners and how they reflect the speaker's values.

   - State feelings honestly.
   - Allow you to accept responsibility.
   - Help you communicate effectively.
   - Show respect for the other person.

3. Brainstorm examples of ineffective statements and point out how these can make people feel defensive (e.g., "You make me mad!").

ACTIVITY: In partners, students role-play a current situation of their own that uses an "I" statement. Be sure to use the students' situations in order to make the role-playing activity believable.

HOMEWORK: Complete "Taking Responsibility with 'I' Statements" activity.

TAKING RESPONSIBILITY WITH "I" STATEMENTS

DIRECTIONS: Change the following accusations into "I" statements.

1. You never call me when you say you will.

2. You lied to me about breaking my stereo.

3. You aren't making any sense!

4. Will you stop annoying me?

5. You never listen to me when I talk to you.

6. If you hadn't dropped the ball, we would have won the game.

7. You didn't tell me the paper was due today. What am I, a mind reader?

8. That's none of your business.

9. Why don't you just leave me alone.

10. You never let me go anywhere.

11. All you do is cry; why don't

12. I'm busy! Go do it yourself.

Adapted from Doody and Dick (1980).

LESSON 10: LISTENING SKILLS
UNIT: COMMUNICATION SKILLS

OBJECTIVE: To demonstrate the ability to listen to others for information and to enhance positive communication.

Group Activity:

1. As a class, determine a working definition of *listening*. Be sure to discuss the difference between hearing and listening. (You can hear something, but not listen to it—i.e., not pay attention to it.)

2. Discuss different components of listening attentively.
   - Body language shows others that you are listening.
   - Asking clarifying questions helps you understand.
   - Paraphrasing helps you clarify what was said.

   If necessary, define *paraphrasing* and practice this with students.

ACTIVITY: Students assess their listening habits using the questionnaire on the next page. Discuss results when finished. An additional activity would be to role-play listening skills using the sample topics given on the following pages.

HOMEWORK: Why is listening one of the most important social skills? Why is it important that people listen to you.

ASSESS YOUR LISTENING SKILLS

Directions: Using the key below, place the correct number on the line provided.

Key: 1 = never · 2 = sometimes · 3 = usually · 4 = always
5 = undecided

_____ 1. I look at the person to whom I am speaking.

_____ 2. I understand most of what is said to me.

_____ 3. There are other things on my mind when I talk to someone.

_____ 4. It is hard to sit quietly and listen.

_____ 5. I get bored with the conversation easily.

_____ 6. I hear more than I listen.

_____ 7. I respond to the other person at the appropriate times.

_____ 8. I interrupt a lot.

_____ 9. I listen only to catch the mistakes of the person talking.

_____ 10. I can't study well with others around or music in the background.

_____ 11. I paraphrase in order to make sure I understand the person speaking.

_____ 12. I often start conversations at inappropriate times.

_____ 13. I am often in conversations when I do not have enough time to talk.

_____ 14. I think about what I need to do, rather than listen to the other person.

_____ 15. I ask questions to clarify what the person is saying.

LISTENING ROLE-PLAY TOPICS

Talk about your idea of the perfect date.

Plan the ideal vacation.

Talk about your favorite movie.

Discuss a time when you were embarrassed.

Tell about the scariest thing that ever happened to you.

What is the best sport and why?

Describe someone you admire and why.

If you had only one week to live, what would you do in that week?

If you could have dinner with three people, who would they be and why did you choose them?

Talk about a situation when you had a great deal of responsibility.

If you had $1,000,000 what would you do with it?

Which charity would you be involved in and why?

If you could live anywhere in the world, where would it be and why?

Did you feel your partner really listened to you? Could your partner report on your answers?

How were you as a listener? Did you and your partner show mutual respect?

LESSON 11: PASSIVE & ACTIVE LISTENING
UNIT: COMMUNICATION SKILLS

OBJECTIVE: To learn and practice the difference between active listening and passive listening in order to become a more attentive listener.

Group Activity:

1. Offer definitions of *passive* and *active listening* and give examples of each.

   - *Passive:* Showing that you are interested without speaking (e.g., nodding head, using facial expressions, etc.)
   - *Active:* Using verbal responses to show that you're listening (e.g., "I see," "Tell me more about...," etc.)

2. Demonstrate both passive and active listening with class volunteers. Emphasize that when we listen actively, we should not pass judgment, but rather show respect and encourage more discussion.

ACTIVITY: In partners, the students practice both passive and active listening. Choose a topic from the listening role-play topics on page 21 and begin discussion with one person as the passive listener. When finished, switch roles and topics, having the other partner play the active listener. Once role-play is finished, distribute the appropriate question sheet asking students about their experience.

HOMEWORK: Which did you enjoy more, being an active or a passive listener? Please explain your answer.

PASSIVE LISTENER RESPONSE SHEET

DIRECTIONS: Answer the following questions based on your conversation today. Be sure to answer them fully and honestly.

1. Did you maintain eye contact with the speaker during the conversation?

2. As a listener, was it hard to understand the person speaking or hard to pay attention to what was being said?

3. Was it difficult to just listen and not respond? Please explain.

4. What facial expressions did you use to show your interest?

5. Did you feel uncomfortable in this role or could you tell if your partner felt uneasy?

6. Was it hard for your partner to keep the conversation going because you were not contributing to it? Please explain.

ACTIVE LISTENER RESPONSE SHEET

DIRECTIONS: Answer the following questions based on your conversation today. Be sure to answer them fully and honestly.

1. Did you find it difficult to be an active listener? If so, what was hard about it?

2. What were the verbal responses you used to show your partner that you were interested?

3. Did you have to concentrate on being an active listener? Please explain.

4. When you encouraged your partner to give more information, did he/she do that easily or did you have to ask several questions?

5. What did you like about being an active listener?

6. Did you find yourself interrupting or cutting your speaker off?

LESSON 12: MISUNDERSTANDINGS
UNIT: COMMUNICATION SKILLS

OBJECTIVE: To recognize an unclear message, and to practice speaking and listening skills to prevent misunderstandings.

Group Activity:

1. As a class, establish a working definition of a *misunderstanding*.

2. Brainstorm things that could lead to a misunderstanding (e.g., not thinking before speaking, drifting in and out of the conversation, being preoccupied).

ACTIVITY: Play "The Gossip Game." Students sit in a circle and the teacher begins by telling the first person a message. Students are required to pass the message on to the next person as accurately as possible. When everyone has received the message, it is announced to the class to test the correctness of communicating in this manner. Repeat as often as students would like. When finished, discuss the reasons that people misunderstand each other. Examples:

- People may be preoccupied and hear only bits and pieces.

- People may hear only what they want to hear.

- Sometimes we distort statements to match our expectations.

- The way a message is presented may cause misinterpretation.

- Speech/articulation difficulties may cause misunderstanding.

You may want the class to give examples of the above reasons.

HOMEWORK: Write about a recent misunderstanding you had and try to figure out what went wrong.

LESSON 13: MIXED MESSAGES
UNIT: COMMUNICATION SKILLS

OBJECTIVE: To recognize and prevent errors in our communication and to practice saying what we mean to say.

Group Activity:

1. Explain that *split communication* happens when we say one thing, but really mean something else.

2. Brainstorm examples of mixed messages. For example, someone says "I don't care" in a sarcastic voice or in a way that is difficult to tell if the person really does or doesn't care.

ACTIVITY: Complete the "Jumbled Jargon" activity on the next page and review answers when finished.

HOMEWORK: Write about a recent incident when someone sent you a mixed message. How could that person have spoken to you differently? Please explain.

JUMBLED JARGON

DIRECTIONS: Read the situations below and identify the mixed messages. On the line provided, tell what you think is really being said.

1. Your friend tells you that your teacher said she would fail the class. Your friend says, "I don't care; she's a mean teacher anyway." What does he really mean to say?

   _____

2. You've been dating someone for a while and he/she has been acting distant. When you ask your partner if everything is all right, he/she says, "Yeah, everything's cool." What does your partner really mean?

   _____

3. You are not very busy and your father gives you some chores to do. You haven't even started doing them when he comes by and says, "There's no rush, we have all day to get these chores done." What does your father really mean?

   _____

4. A friend that your parents don't really like comes by to pick you up. They think she is a bad influence on you. Your mother sends her a cold smile and says, "Have a great time!" What does she really mean?

   _____

5. You need some money to go out on a date. You ask a friend for a loan and she says, "Oh sure, I've got tons of money to give to you, and don't worry about paying me back!" What does your friend mean to say?

   _____

LESSON 14: COMMUNICATION OBSTACLES
UNIT: COMMUNICATION SKILLS

OBJECTIVE: To recognize and avoid using defenses when trying to communicate effectively. To understand the different types of barriers people use when communicating.

Group Activity:

1. Explain *communication roadblocks* as "ways we say things to others that may block communication."

2. Brainstorm examples of communication roadblocks. Examples: arguing, criticizing, making excuses, avoiding the issue, or being sarcastic. (Be sure to provide a working definition of each roadblock to ensure complete understanding.)

ACTIVITY: Pair students for role-playing. Allow them to choose one of the following topics and hold a natural conversation about it. When they have finished the conversation, complete the communication blocks questionnaire on the next page. Use the questionnaire to analyze the conversation. Topics:

- What would you do if you had more free time?
- What law do you think is unfair and explain why?
- If you could change anything about yourself, what would it be?

HOMEWORK: During the day, pay close attention to the person with whom you are having a conversation. Record any communication roadblocks you encounter. Explain the roadblock and what needs to be done to correct it.

COMMUNICATION BLOCKS

QUESTIONNAIRE

DIRECTIONS: Based on your conversation with your partner, please answer the following questions. Check the yes or no column.

YES   NO

____ ____ 1. Did your partner try to persuade you to think differently or argue his/her point by saying something like, "Yes, but..." or "That's not right..."?

____ ____ 2. Did your partner criticize anything you said with, "You're not thinking straight because..."?

____ ____ 3. Did you feel you were being analyzed or that your partner was "reading into" what you were saying and misinterpreting what was said?

____ ____ 4. Did your partner ever say, "Your problem is..."?

____ ____ 5. When faced with a contradiction, did your partner ever become defensive or make excuses for being wrong?

____ ____ 6. Did your partner try to give you advice, even when you did not ask for it?

____ ____ 7. Did you feel that your partner was asking too many questions that you feel were too personal?

____ ____ 8. Did you feel that your partner avoided certain topics by changing the subject or saying, "Forget it."?

____ ____ 9. Was your partner sarcastic in any way or did you feel put down?

____ ____ 10. Did your partner show you respect during the conversation?

On a separate sheet of paper, please write a summary of your conversation and explain why your partner was a good communicator or not. Be sure to give examples of communication blocks that were used.

Adapted from Kramer (1994).

GOOD CHARACTER

LESSON 15: CONVERSATION PIECES
UNIT: COMMUNICATION SKILLS

OBJECTIVE: To start a conversation properly and practice good communication techniques, including body language.

Group Activity:

1. Discuss why proper body language (e.g., eye contact, stance, etc.) is important when having a conversation.

2. Define *small talk* as casual conversation topics we use when starting a conversation. Discuss why we use small-talk.

3. Brainstorm small-talk topics. Give examples if needed (weather, sports, movies, hobbies, etc.).

ACTIVITY:

1. Students complete the conversation evaluation on the next page. When finished, discuss results.

2. Role-play situations on the "Awkward Talk" sheet. Discuss results when finished.

HOMEWORK: If you could start a conversation with a famous person, who would it be? What types of small talk topics would you use during the conversation? Explain what you would say.

RATE YOUR CONVERSATION SKILLS

DIRECTIONS: Evaluate your conversations. Please read each statement and check either "yes," "no," or "sometimes."

When having a conversation, do you

	Yes	Sometimes	No
face the person who is speaking?	_____	_____	_____
maintain eye contact?	_____	_____	_____
respond to what is said?	_____	_____	_____
show respect?	_____	_____	_____
answer all questions?	_____	_____	_____
stay on the topic?	_____	_____	_____
concentrate on other things?	_____	_____	_____
try not to interrupt?	_____	_____	_____
change the conversation topic?	_____	_____	_____
ask questions that may be too personal?	_____	_____	_____
give clear information?	_____	_____	_____
get upset when criticized?	_____	_____	_____
talk about things in an interesting way?	_____	_____	_____
talk to others when you are in a bad mood?	_____	_____	_____
listen passively?	_____	_____	_____
listen actively without disrupting others?	_____	_____	_____
avoid talking to people you do not know?	_____	_____	_____
assume things about the other person?	_____	_____	_____
enjoy having conversations?	_____	_____	_____

Do you think you have good conversation skills? Explain what conversational skills you would like to improve.

AWKWARD TALK

DIRECTIONS: In pairs, practice the following awkward ways to communicate. Use small talk topics such as sports, favorite group, movies, etc.

1. One person stands, while the other sits in a chair.
2. Both people stand facing each other only inches apart.
3. Both people stand back to back.
4. One person stands and the other sits facing the opposite way.
5. One person looks out the window while the other talks.
6. Both people start out standing facing each other, then slowly back up during the conversation.
7. One person talks while the other gets up and walks away.
8. Both people talk at the same time.
9. One person starts the conversation, while the other comments on something else.
10. One person talks and the other does not respond in any way.

Adapted from Toner (1993).

LESSON 16: INTERRUPTION ERUPTION
UNIT: COMMUNICATION SKILLS

OBJECTIVE:

To recognize when we (or someone else) interrupts a conversation and to practice interrupting appropriately.

Group Activity:

1. As a class, determine a definition of *interrupting* as "butting in" or disrupting someone's conversation.

2. Discuss the positive and negative aspects of interrupting a conversation. Ask for examples of when it is appropriate to interrupt (e.g., emergencies).

3. Discuss the importance of entering a conversation without interrupting, as well as why people do interrupt (e.g., they cannot wait to say what is on their minds).

ACTIVITY:

As a class, construct a list of things we need to be aware of when entering a conversation or when we are about to interrupt others.

- *Location:* Are the people talking in a place where there is no one else around?

- *Loudness:* Are they whispering or speaking in a normal tone?

- *Body language:* Do they look upset or do they look relaxed and at ease?

With these factors in mind, complete "Should I Interrupt?" worksheet on the next page.

HOMEWORK:

Have you ever entered a conversation and realized that you shouldn't have? Explain what happened and how you dealt with the embarrassment.

SHOULD I INTERRUPT?

DIRECTIONS: Read the following situations and determine if you should interrupt. On the lines provided, explain why it is okay to interrupt or why you shouldn't.

1. Your friend comes into class looking angry and frustrated. She walks into the room, goes over to another friend and slams her books down on the desk. On top of her books is a piece of paper with an "F" on it. Should you interrupt the two girls as they talk about last period's test?

   _____

   _____

2. Your teacher is talking to another student who is sitting up near the teacher's desk. They seem to be whispering and the student is crying. You are stuck on the assignment and can't do anymore until you ask the teacher. Should you interrupt?

   _____

   _____

3. Two people are outside talking about an upcoming concert. As you walk toward them, they smile and wave. Should you join in on their conversation?

   _____

   _____

4. You are stuck at the movies because your ride never showed up. You don't see a phone in sight. The person behind the ticket counter is talking to his boss. Should you interrupt them to ask to use a phone?

   _____

   _____

COMMUNICATION
QUOTATIONS OF THE WEEK:

"Sticks and stones may break our bones,
but words will break our hearts."
- Robert Fulghum -

"Silent gratitude isn't very much use to anyone."
- G.B. Stern -

"Wisdom is the reward you get for a lifetime of listening
when you'd have preferred to talk."
- Doug Larson -

"Everyone has to think to be polite;
the first impulse is to be impolite."
- Edgar Watson Howe -

"Words are less needful to sorrow than to joy."
- Helen Hunt Jackon -

"Don't be ashamed to say
what you are not ashamed to think."
- Michael de Montaigne -

Teacher tip:
Pin one of the quotations above to a bulletin board and ask students to reflect on what is said, apply it to their thinking and explain if they agree with it. You may have them write about it in their value journals.

RELATIONSHIPS
PART 1: Family and Friends

This is a vital unit in any social skills program, particularly if the program includes students with learning difficulties. In this unit, students learn about the different types of relationships in their lives, with a particular focus on family, friendships, and acquaintances. They will learn how important communication is in a relationship, as well as how to trust someone without being an open target whom others can take advantage of. Students will understand all the positive aspects and the rewards we gain from our relationships, but they will also learn that these rewards cannot be reaped without respect, compassion, and honesty. The unit includes lessons to help with setting and respecting boundaries, dealing with rejection and with peer pressure, being a good friend, and behaving in a respectable manner. Students will learn many strategies that aid in nurturing a healthy relationship.

Part 2 applies these same objectives to dating and romantic relationships.

LESSON 17: DISCOVERING RELATIONSHIPS
UNIT: RELATIONSHIPS

OBJECTIVE: To recognize and define the different relationships in our lives, as well as the value of relationships.

Group Activity:

1. Determine a working definition of *relationships* that encompasses a connection people have between each other.

2. Brainstorm different types of relationships. Once a list is developed, the class describes characteristics of those relationships (why we have them).

3. Discuss how self-esteem is affected by our relationships, how different relationships make you feel, etc.

ACTIVITY: Divide the class into groups of two or three. Distribute a copy of the Golden Rule. Ask groups to modify this and/or develop their own creed for making relationships work. Once the creeds are developed, have groups create a poster to express their idea of healthy relationships.

HOMEWORK: Why is it important to have a relationship with yourself before you have one with anyone else?

THE GOLDEN RULE

Treat others as you would like to be treated.

LESSON 18: FAMILY TRADITIONS
UNIT: RELATIONSHIPS

OBJECTIVE: To identify family traditions and rituals, as well as the values and beliefs of the family.

Group Activity:

1. Define *traditions* as customs that are passed on from one generation to the next and *rituals* as a usual or expected way to act. Discuss why we have traditions and rituals.

2. Brainstorm different family traditions and rituals. Some common responses:

   • Fourth of July picnic.

   • Sunday dinner.

   • Taking the dog for a walk each night.

   • Attending church services each week.

ACTIVITY: Distribute "Traditions and Rituals in My Family" sheet and ask students to fill it out based on their own families. Ask students to share responses when they have completed the activity.

HOMEWORK: What is your favorite family tradition or ritual? Why is this one so important to you?

TRADITIONS AND RITUALS IN MY FAMILY

DIRECTIONS: Fill in the chart below by stating your family's traditions and rituals. Next list the values that are shown and finally, why the tradition or ritual is important to you.

TRADITION/RITUAL	VALUE	IMPORTANCE

LESSON 19: **ALL IN THE FAMILY**
UNIT: RELATIONSHIPS

OBJECTIVE: To help students discover the importance of family in their lives and analyze the roles of different family members in the family relationship.

Group Activity:

1. Discuss how families operate and how each member has a specific role. Touch upon how family members depend upon one another in various situations.

2. Brainstorm situations when family members need each other. Solicit student examples.

3. Discuss when family members turn away or rebel against others in their family and why.

ACTIVITY: Distribute "Family Matters" questionnaire. Students answer questions independently. When the questionnaires have been completed, ask for student volunteers to share answers.

HOMEWORK: How important is your family to you? Explain why.

FAMILY MATTERS

DIRECTIONS: Answer the following questions about your family life. Be sure to answer them honestly. This will help you get a better understanding of youself and your family.

1. Do you participate in family activities? If so, which ones?

2. Do you have family meetings when something important needs to be discussed?

3. Are your family traditions and rituals the same now as they were when you were younger? Are they still important to you?

4. Are you more devoted to your family or your friends? Why?

5. Is your time with your friends more valuable than your time with your family? Is being with your family a burden? Why?

6. Do you talk openly with your family? Why or why not?

7. What values do you hold that are the same as those of your family?

8. What do you want from your family?

LESSON 20: PARENT RELATIONSHIPS
UNIT: RELATIONSHIPS

OBJECTIVE: To understand the role of parents in a family and to discover the importance of parental guidance throughout life.

Group Activity:

1. Talk about the role of parents in families and the importance of that role. Keep in mind that some students may not have both parents in their household.

2. Venting session: Allow students to voice their opinions about their parents. When finished, remind them that they do have parents and some people do not. (Those who do have parents are fortunate.) Finally, ask them to evaluate themselves: What if you became a parent today, how well would you do? Wait for responses.

ACTIVITY: Distribute "Me and My Parents" questionnaire. Ask students to evaluate their relationship with their parents. Encourage them to answer the questions open-mindedly.

HOMEWORK: How can you improve your relationship with your parents? Please explain.

ME AND MY PARENTS

DIRECTIONS: Answer the questions below on a separate piece of paper. This is an effort for you to think about your relationship with your parents. Please answer the questions openly and honestly.

1. When do you think parents should stop telling their kids what to do?

2. What values do you think are important for both parents and their children?

3. At what age should young people be allowed to date?

4. When should young people be allowed to go to unchaperoned parties?

5. Do your parents try to act like teenagers? Why do you think this happens?

6. What is hard about talking to your parents?

7. Is it enough for your parents to tell you how they feel or do you think they need to show their feelings?

8. What is the best thing about your parents?

9. Do you think parents should allow their children to choose religion or not? Please explain why?

10. What annoys you the most about your parents?

On a another piece of paper, try to answer the above questions from your parents' point of view or ask your parents the same questions and record their answers. Talk with your parents about how they felt toward their parents.

LESSON 21: FAMILY FEUD
UNIT: RELATIONSHIPS

OBJECTIVE: To help students recognize when family conflicts are building and how to pinpoint what may trigger a conflict.

Group Activity:

1. Brainstorm things that can cause conflicts in families.
   - Money.
   - House rules.
   - Different values.
   - The way family members treat each other.

2. Discuss the fact that those who are older in the family are setting examples for younger members in both behavior and decisions. Emphasize that understanding what is important to the members of your family, as well as what bothers them, can be very useful information for understanding the effect family members have on each other.

ACTIVITY:

1. Independently, ask students to complete an in-class journal. Ask them to think about their families and write a sentence about their relationship with each member of their immediate household. When finished, ask them to list the things that bother them about their family.

3. Solicit student volunteers to share what they feel could cause a conflict.

2. Role-play the situations that are volunteered. Accentuate the students' open-mindedness in trying to avoid conflicts.

HOMEWORK: Is there a recent family conflict that you can try to resolve?
Please explain the conflict and what can be done.

LESSON 22: FAMILY CONFLICT RESOLUTION
UNIT: RELATIONSHIPS

OBJECTIVE: To discover possible solutions for family conflicts.

Group Activity:

1. Review the things that can cause conflicts in families.
    - Curfews.
    - Types of friends.
    - Jealousy between siblings.

2. Discuss how conflicts in families can be resolved.
    - Family meetings.
    - Outside counseling.
    - Parents allowing their child to speak and really listening.
    - Using a family mediator to ensure both sides are listening.

3. Ask students to get into groups of two or three and choose one of the family conflicts on the next page. Ask them to role-play the situation and discuss the results when finished.

HOMEWORK: Describe a family conflict from a television show or a movie you have seen recently. Help the people resolve their conflict.

FAMILY CONFLICT ROLE-PLAYS

DIRECTIONS: Choose one of the following situations and try to resolve the family conflict by making suggestions.

1. Your friends want you to go to a party that will be unchaperoned, but your parents won't let you go.

2. It is Thursday night and you have school tomorrow. Your curfew is 10:00 p.m. and the movie you've been dying to see starts at 9:00 p.m. You think it's unfair that your parents won't let you go.

3. Your sister has "borrowed" your favorite sweater without asking and you saw her leave the house with it on. You confront her.

4. There is a family gathering at your house and your mother asks you to help clean the house. You've already done your chores and your brother hasn't lifted a finger. You were asked because you are older.

5. It seems like your younger sister gets all the breaks and you seem to get in trouble for every little thing.

6. It is report card day and you are failing math class. Your parents told you that you cannot play sports until your grades improve. You are the captain of the team.

Be sure to take all sides into consideration. If you are playing a parent, try to see things from a parent's point of view, etc.

LESSON 23: BUILDING TRUST
UNIT: RELATIONSHIPS

OBJECTIVE:

To help students understand whom to trust and whom not to trust, as well as deepen their trust in others.

Group Activity:

1. Develop a working definition of *trust* to include placing confidence in someone and being able to depend on him/her.

2. Discuss the value of being trustworthy in order to be able to trust others. Be sure to include what other values trust shows: being honest, showing respect, taking responsibility in the relationship, etc.

3. Brainstorm ways people show that they can be trusted as well as ways they break trust. What types of things do people do that show we can't trust them?

ACTIVITY:

1. Ask students to write about a secret they are keeping right now. When the secrets are written, ask for volunteers to talk about what they have written. Challenge them to trust the class.

2. Complete "I Trust...." activity on the next page. Discuss results when finished. This may be done either independently or together.

HOMEWORK:

Write about the person you trust the most and explain why you hold so much confidence in him/her.

I TRUST ....

DIRECTIONS: Answer the following questions about people you trust.

1. Name someone you would trust to help you with your homework.

   _____

   _____

2. Name someone you would trust to listen when you have a problem and to give advice only when you ask for it.

   _____

   _____

3. Name someone you would trust to come and help if your car broke down.

   _____

   _____

4. Name someone you would trust to tell your deepest secret to, knowing that person would not tell anyone else.

   _____

   _____

5. Name someone you would trust to stand up for you when you are being teased by others.

   _____

   _____

6. Name someone you would trust to point out something that may embarrass you.

_____

_____

ANALYZE YOURSELF

1. Can the people listed above trust you? If so, what have you done to prove to them that you can be trusted?

_____

_____

2. What do people trust the most about you, what types of qualities?

_____

_____

3. Have you ever done anything that caused someone to lose trust in you? If so, what did you do and how did you earn their trust back?

_____

_____

LESSON 24: HONESTY IS THE BEST POLICY
UNIT: RELATIONSHIPS

OBJECTIVE: To help students evaluate how honest they are and guide them on how to become more honest with themselves and others.

Group Activity:

1. Develop a working definition of *honesty* to include not only telling the truth, but also doing and saying things without deception.

2. Discuss the values shown when we are honest: respect, responsibility, trustworthiness, etc.

3. Brainstorm reasons why people are dishonest. Examples: fear, personal gain, anger, pressure from others, nervousness, etc.

ACTIVITY:

1. In a short paragraph, students describe a situation when they have been dishonest with someone. Once completed, put aside for homework assignment.

2. Take honesty survey on the next page to assess how truthful we are. Discuss results when completed.

HOMEWORK: Write a letter to the person to whom you have been dishonest. (From the in-class activity, above.) Explain why you did what you did and sincerely apologize. You will be taking the first steps toward rebuilding trust.

HOW HONEST ARE YOU?

*DIRECTIONS: Answer the following survey to measure your honesty. Either place a **Y** for yes or **N** for no on the line before each statement.*

_____ 1. Have you ever cheated on a test?

_____ 2. Would you change your I.D. to get into a dance club for people 18 and older?

_____ 3. Have you ever purposely not given the whole story to someone for fear of getting in trouble?

_____ 4. Did you ever sneak out of the house?

_____ 5. Would you steal food if your family had no money and was hungry?

_____ 6. Would you go through a red light if it was 1:00 A.M., there was no one around and you were late getting home?

_____ 7. Would you cheat on your income tax if you could?

_____ 8. Would you correct a cashier who gave you more change than you should have gotten back?

_____ 9. If you were small for your age, would you try to get into a movie for the children's price?

_____ 10. Would you turn in a friend you saw stealing something from a store?

_____ 11. Have you ever made plans with one friend and then made an excuse to get out of it because you got a better invitation?

GOOD CHARACTER

LESSON 25: CHARACTERISTICS OF FRIENDSHIP
UNIT: RELATIONSHIPS

OBJECTIVE: To examine the characteristics and values of a good friend.

Group Activity:

1. Define *friendship* as being attached or bonded to someone by affection, caring and respect.

2. Brainstorm characteristics of a good friend and the values that should be practiced in friendship: honesty, respect, good listener, fun, caring, etc.

3. Discuss negative aspects of friendship: gossiping, loss of friends, loneliness, popularity vs. friendship, etc.

ACTIVITY: Students brainstorm their own list of characteristics of a good friend. Ask them to keep in mind that they are creating the perfect friend. When the lists are completed, students make friend collages by cutting out pictures and words from magazines that describe the perfect friend.

HOMEWORK: Describe what makes you a good friend. Which of the characteristics from today's activity do you show as a friend? Please explain.

LESSON 26: BEING A GOOD FRIEND
UNIT: RELATIONSHIPS

OBJECTIVE: To help students recognize their beliefs regarding what a friendship should be, as well understand why they need to show the qualities of a friend in order to have friends.

Group Activity:

Discuss the differences between friendship and popularity. Emphasize the need to go slow when building a friendship and the role that trust plays in that friendship.

ACTIVITY: Complete "What Is Important in a Friendship?" activity on the next page. Students will evaluate themselves as friends, as well as what is important in a friendship. Discuss responses when finished. Students come up with a "Friendship Motto"—a saying that describes how they feel about friendship. Examples: "Good friends are friends for life!," "Things are better when you have a friend to share them with," etc.

HOMEWORK: Write about a friend who shares the same values as you. Why do you have a friendship with this person?

WHAT IS IMPORTANT IN A FRIENDSHIP?

DIRECTIONS: Answer the following questions as honestly as possible to see what is important to you in a friendship.

1. Your friend has an awful new haircut and thinks it is cool. Do you tell your friend your honest opinion or do you say something nice to spare hard feelings?

   _____

   _____

2. What bothers you more about friends: when they gossip, make fun of you because it will be funny to others, or when they don't listen?

   _____

   _____

3. What is most important to you in a friendship: honesty, loyalty or caring?

   _____

   _____

4. What would you do if your best friend started taking drugs?

   _____

   _____

5. If you and your friend both wanted the one position left on the soccer team, would you give it up or try your best for that spot on the team?

   _____

   _____

6. What are the four most important qualities that a best friend must have?

_____

_____

7. Is it important for your friends to share your beliefs and values? Explain.

_____

_____

8. Is it important to back up a friend who did something wrong, like stealing?

_____

_____

9. Is it important to you to hang out with the popular crowd? Explain.

_____

_____

10. Would you make friends with someone who was made fun of by the popular kids? Explain.

_____

_____

_____

GOOD CHARACTER

LESSON 27: TYPES OF FRIENDS
UNIT: RELATIONSHIPS

OBJECTIVE: To help students analyze their current friendships to determine if they are healthy relationships and to help students recognize characteristics of people who are not friends.

Group Activity:

1. Brainstorm characteristics of an unhealthy friendship. Discuss why people act in these ways.

2. On a separate piece of paper, ask students to list things they have done that do not show good friendship.

ACTIVITY: Discuss the types of friends described on the next pages and ask students to write down things to do to help these undesirable friends change their ways.

HOMEWORK: Write about one of your friends that may fit one of the types of friends discussed in today's activity. What attracted you to that person enough to seek him/her out as a friend?

CAST OF CHARACTERS
FRIENDS SHOULD NOT BE....

Possessive:
- wanting to be with their friends all the time.
- jealous when their friends spend time with others.
- unwilling to give friends time to themselves.

CHANGES: _____

_____

_____

Followers:
- agree with anything their friends say.
- just go along with the crowd.
- offer no suggestions or opinions.

CHANGES: _____

_____

_____

Whiners:
- constantly complain about anything and everything.
- almost always have something negative to say.
- are not happy unless there is a problem.

CHANGES: _____

_____

_____

GOOD CHARACTER

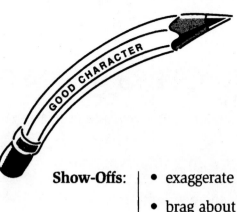

Show-Offs:
- exaggerate stories to impress people.
- brag about how great they are.
- talk about themselves: every sentence starts with "I" and ends with "me."

CHANGES: _____

_____

_____

Two-Faced:
- talk behind friends' backs and then are nice to them to their faces.
- have friends because they gossip about others.
- cannot be trusted.

CHANGES: _____

_____

_____

Users:
- make friends with the popular people, then dump old friends.
- treat other friends like they do not exist.
- call their old friends when popular people are not around.

CHANGES: _____

_____

_____

LESSON 28: SETTING BOUNDARIES
UNIT: RELATIONSHIPS

OBJECTIVE: To help students understand control and why others control us, and to help students understand how to set boundaries in a relationship.

Group Activity:

1. Define *control* as having power over another person.

2. Brainstorm ways people have control over us.
   - Telling who you can be friends with.
   - Saying that if you don't do something, he/she won't be friends with you.

3. Define *boundaries* as setting limits for what you will put up with from others. Give examples of boundaries people set and ask for student examples. Focus on how realistic these boundaries are.

ACTIVITY: Divide the class into groups. Ask them to describe a friend who has been controlling. They should come up with a name, specifically explain what this person does to other friends, and set up a plan to help the other friends deal with the one who is controlling others. Be sure that they set realistic boundaries. When finished, students share projects with the class.

HOMEWORK: Have you ever been controlled by a friend? Was this person a friend by showing you respect and respecting your boundaries? Please explain.

LESSON 29: FRIENDS WHO INFLUENCE US
UNIT: RELATIONSHIPS

OBJECTIVE: To help students increase their awareness of how their behavior can be influenced by their friends.

Group Activity:

1. Define *influence* as someone having enough power over another to convince them to act in a certain way.

2. Brainstorm ways that others can influence us.
   - Sneaking out of the house.
   - Stealing something because it's cool.
   - Doing drugs.

3. Discuss the following statement and ask for feelings about it: "The more you spend time with your friends, the more you become like them."

ACTIVITY: Answer the questionnaire about friends on the next page. Analyze your choices of friends to see how much they influence you and the decisions you make.

HOMEWORK: If you could choose any famous person as a friend, who would it be and why? Please explain what kind of influence this person would be on you.

THE POWER OF FRIENDS

DIRECTIONS: Using a separate sheet of paper, answer the following questions about your friends.

1. Who are your friends? Please list them.
2. Why did you choose these people to become friends with?
3. What makes your friends cool? (Clothes, others they know, share the same values, sports, etc.)
4. Have you ever felt pressured by your friends to do something you knew wasn't right? Please explain.
5. How are your friends like you? How are they different from you?
6. Do you find it hard to be alone or to make decisions? If so, what is hard about it?
7. Have you changed your style of clothing or other behavior because of how your friends act? Please explain.
8. Do you sometimes act a certain way because you are afraid your friends won't like you or hang around with you anymore? How?

LESSON 30: TRIANGLE FRIENDSHIPS
UNIT: RELATIONSHIPS

OBJECTIVE: To help students understand the problems that can occur when three people develop a close friendship.

Group Activity:

1. Define *triangle friendships* as those friendships that are developed with three people.

2. Brainstorm the problems that can occur when there are three people in a close friendship.

   • Two persons can talk about the third person behind that person's back.

   • One person is almost always left out.

   • Two of the friends can become closer with each other than with the third.

ACTIVITY: Divide the class into groups of three and role-play using the situations on the next page. When completed, ask students to fill out the questionnaire about their role-play.

HOMEWORK: Have you ever been involved in a triangle friendship? If so, explain what kind of relationship it was as well as any problems you may have had.

TRIANGLE FRIENDSHIP ROLE-PLAYS

DIRECTIONS: Choose one of the following situations and assign each person in your group to a role. Discuss the situation with the others as if it has happened to you. Be sure to be realistic in your conversation.

1. You just found out that one of your two friends has been talking about you to the other behind your back.

2. Lately, you have noticed that your other two friends have been spending more time together and less with you.

3. Your two other friends have decided to go to a concert together—the concert you've been dying to go to—and they did not invite you.

4. One of your friends likes the same person who your other friend likes and asks you not to tell.

5. One friend is mad at the other and they both come to talk to you about the situation. Both want your advice and they both talk about the other negatively behind that person's back.

CAN YOU HANDLE A TRIANGLE FRIENDSHIP?

DIRECTIONS: Answer the following questions based on your role-playing situation.

1. How hard was it for you to try to be friends with two others at the same time?

2. What was the problem in your situation?

3. Was the problem one that could easily be solved or was it one that could happen again?

4. What were the emotions you were feeling in your role?

5. Do you think that three people can maintain a close friendship? Please explain.

6. Did anything happen that might permanently damage the friendship? If so, what was the situation?

LESSON 31: PLATONIC RELATIONSHIPS
UNIT: RELATIONSHIPS

OBJECTIVE: To help students recognize the difference between a romance and a friendship between a male and a female.

Group Activity:

1. Define a *platonic friendship* as guys and girls being just friends, without a romantic involvement.

2. Ask students if they think guys and girls can just be friends. Do you find it easier to be friends with someone of the opposite sex? Why?

3. Brainstorm some of the problems that may accompany a platonic friendship.
   - Others teasing about the relationship.
   - Other friends pressuring the two to go out.
   - Possibly a more emotional involvement.
   - Jealousy on the part of one's boyfriend/girlfriend.

ACTIVITY: Divide the class into two groups. Ask one group to take the side for platonic relationships and the other to take the side against them. Debate the issues that come up when males and females are just friends. Ask students to cite examples of people they know with this type of relationship.

HOMEWORK: Have you ever had a platonic friendship? If so, please explain its benefits and drawbacks. If not, do you think you could handle one? Please explain.

LESSON 32: ACQUAINTANCE OR FRIEND?
UNIT: RELATIONSHIPS

OBJECTIVE: To recognize the difference between an acquaintance and a friend.

Group Activity:

1. Define *acquaintance* as someone you know in a casual way, i.e., you are not emotionally attached to that person.

2. Brainstorm the names of people in the school or community who are known as acquaintances. Examples: neighbors, people to whom we just say hello, teachers, parents' friends, etc.

3. Discuss why certain people are acquaintances and not friends. Emphasize that not everyone we are friendly to are friends. The term "friend" is tossed out too frequently and often people who are not true friends are labeled as such.

ACTIVITY: In-class journal: describe a time you treated someone like your friend and overstepped the boundaries of your relationship. For example, you acted like one of your teachers was a friend and got hurt because they didn't act like your friend. Describe the emotions and how you dealt with them.

HOMEWORK: Do you have more friends or more acquaintances? Why do you think that is so?

The Power of Social Skills in Character Development | **Relationships**

LESSON 33: FRIENDSHIP ANALYSIS
UNIT: RELATIONSHIPS

OBJECTIVE: To have students analyze their friendships and discover any changes they made or can make.

Group Activity:

1. Review the differences between true friends and those people who are acquaintances.

2. Discuss how difficult it is to maintain lifetime friends: the emotional commitment, problems that can occur, the importance of values in friendship, etc.

ACTIVITY: Complete the friendship analysis on the next pages to assess students' view of their friendships. Discuss the results when finished.

HOMEWORK: Describe a good friend you have right now and the values you share with him/her.

FINAL ANALYSIS

DIRECTIONS: Answer the following questions about your attitude toward friendships. Be sure to be honest.

1. What are the most important qualities in a friendship?

   _____

   _____

2. In your opinion, what is a true friend?

   _____

   _____

3. Do you now feel that you have as many friends as you did in the beginning of this unit? Please explain.

   _____

   _____

4. What values are important in a friendship and do your current friends have these qualities?

   _____

   _____

5. Are any of your friendships ending? If so, please explain what is happening.

   _____

   _____

6. Have you become more cautious with your decision to become friends with someone?

   _____

   _____

7. Is it hard or easy for you to trust others? Please explain why.

   _____

   _____

8. How are your friendships tested? Do others try to break up the friendship? Do you have a lot of fights? And so forth.

_____

_____

9. Do your parents like or dislike your friends? Why?

_____

_____

10. Are your friends the type of people who will accept you for who you are?

_____

_____

11. Have others told you that you have changed? If so, in what ways?

_____

_____

12. How do you feel about limiting the number of your friends? Is this something you feel you will do now?

_____

_____

13. If there are friends you now realize are not your friends, how will you go about ending the friendship?

_____

_____

14. Do you have a best friend? If so, describe him/her and why you feel so strongly about this relationship.

_____

_____

15. Have any of your friends ever gotten you in trouble? Please explain.

_____

_____

16. What will you look for in a friend in the future?

_____

_____

FRIENDSHIP

QUOTATIONS OF THE WEEK:

"What is a friend? I will tell you.
It is a person with whom you dare to be yourself."
- Frank Crane -

"Chance makes our relatives but choice makes our friends."
- Delille

"The only way to have a friend is to be one."
- Ralph Waldo Emerson -

"A real friend will tell you when
you have spinach stuck in your teeth."
- E. C. McKenzie -

"A real friend warms you by his presence,
trusts you with his secrets,
and remembers you in his prayers."
- E. C. McKenzie -

"Never trust a friend who deserts you in a pinch."
- Aesop -

"Faithful friends are hard to find."
- Richard Banfield -

"What do we live for, if it is not to make life
less difficult for each other?"
- George Eliot -

Teacher tip:
Pin one of the quotations to a bulletin board
and ask students to reflect on what is said,
apply it to their thinking, and explain if
they agree with it. You may have them write
about it in their value journals.

RELATIONSHIPS
PART 2: Dating and Romantic Relationships

This section extends the unit objectives to dating and romantic relationships. The lessons are designed to help students determine if they are ready for dating, clarify their values and expectations in a dating situation, understand appropriate dating practices, cope with awkward dating situations, respond to peer pressure, and deal with the feelings that accompany rejection or the end of a romantic relationship.

LESSON 34: AM I READY TO DATE?
UNIT: RELATIONSHIPS

OBJECTIVE: To help students determine if they are ready for dating, how to approach someone they are attracted to, and how to make a good first impression.

Group Activity:

1. Discuss how we know if we are interested in someone (first encounters, meeting someone, etc.).

    - Eye contact.

    - Smiles.

    - Pleasant remarks.

2. Define *attraction* as something about someone that makes you want to pursue some type of relationship with that person.

3. Brainstorm conversation topics that can start a conversation with someone in whom you are interested.

    - Talk about where you've seen them: mall, school, etc.

    - Movies you've seen recently.

    - Compliment the person on what they are wearing.

DON'T:

   - Talk about your problems.

   - Ask questions that are too personal.

   - Come on too strong; they may be scared away.

ACTIVITY: Pair students for role-playing. Give them a topic from the next page and ask them to practice their conversational skills and body language when talking to someone they are attracted to. (Be sure to monitor body language for nervousness and appropriate topics.)

HOMEWORK: How do you know when you are attracted to someone?

FIRST-MEETING ROLE-PLAYS

You've had your eye on someone at school, and you've finally got up the nerve to talk to him/her. What will you say?

You are out at the mall with your friends and you find that you have an interest in the person who works at your favorite record store. What will you say to start a conversation?

You are on a trip with your parents and the people staying in the room next door have a son/daughter your age. How will you start a conversation?

You and your friends go to the movies and you notice the person behind the ticket counter. This person looks familiar to you, but you are not sure if it's from school that you've seen him/her. What will you say to start a conversation?

TIPS: Make sure that you are positive, try to stay calm, and most importantly, be yourself!

LESSON 35: WHAT DO YOU LOOK FOR?
UNIT: RELATIONSHIPS

OBJECTIVE: To help students determine what is important when they are attracted to someone.

Group Activity:

1. Discuss the things that attract people to each other.
   - Physical factors: how a person looks.
   - Behavior: how a person acts.
2. Brainstorm things that make us want to get to know someone better (e.g., warmth, sincerity, sense of humor, looks). Discuss the positive and negative aspects of the things on the list.

ACTIVITY: Divide the class into groups of two or three. Distribute the "Perfect Date" sheet on the next page and ask each group to come up with the ideal person to date.

HOMEWORK: What do you look for in someone to date? Explain your answer.

THE PERFECT DATE

DIRECTIONS: As a group, answer the following questions in order to create the perfect date. Keep in mind that this is unrealistic and no one is perfect. This is just one way for you to determine what you look for in others.

1. What would the person look like or do looks not matter?

_____

_____

2. What types of interests or hobbies would this person have?

_____

_____

3. Where would this person live?

_____

_____

4. Are the parents wealthy or poor?

_____

_____

5. What are this person's background and religion?

_____

_____

6. What values does he/she hold?

_____

_____

7. Is the person outgoing or shy?

_____

_____

8. What extracurricular activities does the person participate in?

_____

_____

9. What types of things would you have in common? (music, movies, clothes, etc.)

_____

_____

LESSON 36: ACCEPTABLE DATING PRACTICES
UNIT: **RELATIONSHIPS**

OBJECTIVE: To help students determine and understand appropriate dating practices.

Group Activity:

1. As a class, brainstorm the latest dating trends.
   - Where to go and what to do.
   - Who pays and what is okay to do on a date (how to act).

2. Distribute the dating guideline questionnaire on the next page. Give students enough time to complete the questionnaire, then talk about the results.

ACTIVITY: As a class and based on the questionnaire, create a poster: "Top 10 Reasons to Date Me." You may wish to do this activity in groups. Examples:

- I don't smoke.
- I am respectful.
- I'm fun and like to have a good time.

HOMEWORK: Talk about the best date you've ever had.

HOW I FEEL ABOUT DATING

DIRECTIONS: Answer the following questions about dating. Be sure to be honest and state how you really feel.

1. At what age is it appropriate to start dating?

   _____

   _____

2. How should a couple decide where to go out on a date?

   _____

   _____

3. Is it okay for a female to ask a male out on a date?

   _____

   _____

4. Who should pay for a date?

   _____

   _____

5. Should people date only those who are of the same ethnic background, religion, and age? Why or why not?

   _____

   _____

6. How late should teenagers be allowed to stay out, and is it okay to date every night?

   _____

   _____

7. How do you ask someone out on a date? What do you say?

_____

_____

8. How should you turn down someone who has asked you for a date?

_____

_____

9. How far should people go on the first date?

_____

_____

10. How would you handle it if your date was being disrespectful and asking you to do more than you want?

_____

_____

11. Is it okay to assume that once you've gone out on a date with someone, that you are now steadily dating? Explain.

_____

_____

LESSON 37: ROMANTIC RELATIONSHIPS
UNIT: RELATIONSHIPS

OBJECTIVE: To help students understand romantic relationships and recognize the importance of commitment and love in a meaningful relationship.

Group Activity:

1. Define *love* as an emotional attachment to someone through affection and respect.

2. Brainstorm the components of a romantic relationship:

   • Values: respect, responsibility, honesty, trust, etc.

   • Self-esteem: You cannot love another until you love yourself.

   • Love is a commitment made to another.

   • Love cannot come on demand—It has to be given to be received.

ACTIVITY: Divide the class into groups and give each group a piece of posterboard. At the top students should write, "Love is...." Ask students to answer the statement in as many ways as possible. (Examples: holding hands, doing things together, etc.)

HOMEWORK: Have you ever been in love with someone? Please describe the experience, including how you felt. What was it about the person that made you love him/her?

LESSON 38: WHAT DO I DO NOW?
UNIT: RELATIONSHIPS

OBJECTIVE: To continue learning about commitment and to recognize difficult situations in romantic relationships.

Group Activity:

1. Review lists from the appropriate dating practices lesson.

2. Ask students if they have ever been in an awkward dating situation. Ask for volunteers to answer or turn this into an in-class journal.

ACTIVITY: Pair students for role-play situations. Ask pairs to choose one of the awkward dating situations on the next page and act it out. Discuss results when finished.

HOMEWORK: Have you ever been in a awkward position with someone you were dating? Please explain.

AWKWARD DATING SITUATIONS

1. Your best friend just told you that he/she has feelings deeper than friendship for you.

2. Your parents do not like your new boyfriend/girlfriend and they forbid you to see each other anymore.

3. Your boyfriend/girlfriend becomes very jealous when you spend time with your friends.

4. You are out with your boyfriend/girlfriend and he/she brought along some liquor.

5. The person you are dating tends to put his/her hands on you too much when you are together.

6. You found out that your boyfriend/girlfriend likes someone else.

7. Your boyfriend/girlfriend accuses you of flirting with other people when you have not.

8. Your boyfriend/girlfriend is ready for a more sexual relationship and you are not.

LESSON 39: JEALOUSY AND TRUST
UNIT: RELATIONSHIPS

OBJECTIVE: To help students understand the meaning of jealousy: where it comes from and how to manage this emotion in order to trust the other person in the romantic relationship.

Group Activity:

1. Define *jealousy* as a feeling of fear of the loss of another's love to someone else. (Defined in the context of the unit.)

2. Discuss why we have jealous feelings:
   - Lack of attention from mate.
   - Lack of affection.
   - Low self-worth (wondering why he/she is with you).

3. Brainstorm things we can do when we feel jealous.
   - Talk with your partner.
   - Figure out exactly what is making you feel jealous.
   - Ask: Am I being irrational? Are my fears getting in the way?
   - Stay calm: Being angry or violent won't solve the problem.

ACTIVITY: Distribute the handout of questions on the next page. Ask students to answer the questions to discover how they feel about jealousy and healthy relationships.

HOMEWORK: Have you ever been jealous in a relationship? If so, how did you handle it?

GREEN WITH ENVY

DIRECTIONS: Answer the following relationship questions about jealousy. Do you know what is needed for a healthy relationship?

1. How do you know when you are feeling jealous?

   _____

   _____

2. Do you sometimes feel other emotions when you are jealous?

   _____

   _____

3. I think jealousy is....

   _____

   _____

4. What are some of the things that make you jealous?

   _____

   _____

5. Why is it important to talk about jealous feelings with your partner?

   _____

   _____

6. Are you afraid your partner will break up with you if you have jealous feelings? Why?

_____

_____

7. Do you believe that you can be trusted?

_____

_____

8. What kinds of things make you feel like you cannot trust your boyfriend/girlfriend?

_____

_____

9. How do you feel when your partner is jealous?

_____

_____

10. How do you act when you are jealous? What can these feelings do to your relationship?

_____

_____

LESSON 40: EXPECTATIONS AND PERCEPTIONS
UNIT: RELATIONSHIPS

OBJECTIVE: To help students learn to set realistic expectations in their relationships and become more aware of not only their perceptions of others, but also of others' perceptions of them.

Group Activity:

1. Define *expectations* as the things we believe will happen to us, what we expect.

2. Brainstorm expectations we have in relationships: trust, loyalty, honesty, respect, comfort, etc.

3. Define *perceptions* as how we see things and others.

4. Discuss how our perception of ourselves can have an effect on setting our expectations. For example, if you see yourself as a warm, beautiful person, you may expect others to be the same way. This may not be realistic.

ACTIVITY: Ask students to fold a piece of paper vertically. On one side, have them list heir expectations in a relationship. When lists are finished, ask them to put a star next to those that are realistic. On the other side of the paper, ask students to list how they perceive themselves. When finished, star those things that they feel others see in them. Discuss answers when finished.

HOMEWORK: Complete "Expectations & Perceptions" questions.

EXPECTATIONS & PERCEPTIONS

DIRECTIONS: Answer the following questions about your expectations as well as your perceptions. Do you need to change the way you think?

1. What values are most important to you?

   _____

   _____

2. Do you expect to get married and have children some day?

   _____

   _____

3. What qualities do you expect from your partner?

   _____

   _____

4. Do you think that it is okay to flirt a little when you are committed to someone else? Explain.

   _____

   _____

5. Name the four most important things about you.

   _____

   _____

6. Do others see the same things in you and let you know them?

_____

_____

7. How do others see you (besides your friends)?

_____

_____

8. Do you expect others to criticize you for things?

_____

_____

9. Do you get upset when others criticize you? Why?

_____

_____

10. What is required for you and your partner to have a healthy relationship? What are the important things you see in your partner?

_____

_____

LESSON 41: PEER PRESSURE
UNIT: RELATIONSHIPS

OBJECTIVE: To increase students' awareness of how their lives are influenced by those who pressure them, and to understand what peer pressure is and to recognize when it is happening.

Group Activity:

1. Define *peer pressure* as when friends or others your own age push you into doing things you do not want to do.

2. Discuss the positive and negative aspects of peer pressure and how difficult it is to make decisions.

3. Brainstorm things that people are pressured about: Getting good grades, drugs, clothing choices, sports, sex, etc.

ACTIVITY: Complete "Challenging Peer Pressure" on the next page and discuss the results when finished.

HOMEWORK: Write about a time you were pressured into doing something you knew wasn't right.

CHALLENGING PEER PRESSURE

DIRECTIONS: Answer each of the questions below to better understand your feelings about peer pressure. Remember to be honest in order to help with your awareness.

1. Have you ever done anything because "everyone else was doing it"? What?

   _____

   _____

2. Which of your values were violated with the situation above?

   _____

   _____

3. Why did you give in to the pressure of your friends?

   _____

   _____

4. Have you ever done anything against your better judgment because you felt the cool people would then like you? What was it?

   _____

   _____

5. Have you ever been pressured by your boyfriend/girlfriend? Explain.

   _____

   _____

6. Did you give in to his/her pressure because you were afraid he/she wouldn't like you anymore?

_____

_____

7. Why is it hard for you to say no when you know the activity is wrong?

_____

_____

8. Do you ever think about the consequences of your actions?

_____

_____

9. Have you ever been pressured into smoking, sex, drugs, etc.? Which ones?

_____

_____

10. Have you ever been pressured by your friends in a positive way? Explain.

_____

_____

LESSON 42: SURVIVING A BREAK-UP
UNIT: RELATIONSHIPS

OBJECTIVE: To help students deal with an unhealthy relationship: how to recognize it, how to end it, and how to respond to rejection.

Group Activity:

1. Define *rejection* as when someone is turned away by another, not wanting to be associated with someone anymore.

2. Brainstorm signs that the relationship is an unhealthy one.
   - Frequent arguing over little things.
   - Frequent jealousy.
   - Your partner keeps secrets from you.
   - You don't feel comfortable with your partner.

3. Discuss how to prepare for a break-up. Remember that rarely do both partners feel the same intensity in a relationship. One may feel more attached than the other. What should you do?
   - Be honest with your partner about your feelings.
   - Be kind.
   - Don't blame yourself or your partner.
   - Think about how your partner feels.
   - Don't be talked into anything you don't feel is right, prepare for the hurt.

ACTIVITY: Divide the class into groups and ask them to come up with a list of things to do to help with the healing process after a break-up. Examples may be: stick to a routine, keep busy, spend time with friends, ask for help if needed (someone to talk to), etc. Discuss student lists when finished and ask for volunteers to talk about their experiences.

HOMEWORK: Have you ever experienced a break-up? If so, explain how you felt and what happened.

RELATIONSHIP
QUOTATIONS OF THE WEEK:

"There is nothing greater in life than loving another
and being loved in return,
for loving is the ultimate of experiences."
- Leo F. Buscaglia -

"True love is like a ghost.
Everybody talks about it but few have seen it."
- Doris Day -

"Love is an itchy feeling around the heart that
you can't scratch."
- Alexander Magoun -

"Love is a friendship that has caught fire...
If you have love in your life,
it can make up for a great many things you lack."
- Ann Landers -

"We grow for people who believe in us,
who trust us, who love us."
- Unknown -

"Let us always meet each other with a smile,
for the smile is the beginning of love."
- Mother Teresa -

Teacher tip:
*Pin one of the quotations to a bulletin board
and ask students to reflect on what is said,
apply it to their thinking and explain if they
agree with it. You may have them write
about it in their value journals.*

UNIT IV

CRITICISM AND ATTITUDES

This unit accentuates students' ability to understand what criticism is, why someone would give criticism, and why we must respect someone enough to listen to what he/she is saying. The students understand that listening to criticism is difficult, yet it can be a good way to learn about themselves. Students will be able to distinguish between constructive criticism and put downs, as well as how to listen without getting angry. They will be able to criticize a person's actions, not the person. Self-criticism is covered in this unit in order for the students to explore their needs and how they can motivate themselves positively. Students realize that it takes courage and self-discipline to accept limitations in order to discover their assets.

LESSON 43: CRITICISM KNOW-HOW
UNIT: CRITICISM AND ATTITUDES

OBJECTIVE: To help students achieve a greater awareness of what criticism is and the different types of criticism.

Group Activity:

1. Define *criticism* as telling someone that you don't like what he/she did or said and explaining why.

2. Brainstorm the different types of criticism and define if necessary.

   - Constructive criticism.

   - Put-downs.

   - Commands.

   - Suggestions.

3. Discuss certain rules that should be followed when we criticize someone.

   - Express the criticism using an "I" statement.

   - Be sure to criticize things people CAN change.

   - Be sure not to insult the person.

   - Be positive.

   - Attack the issue, not the person.

ACTIVITY: Divide the class into groups and ask them to devise a list of things people should be criticized for. Once lists are finished, discuss the results and talk about being sensitive to others' feelings. (THINK BEFORE YOU SPEAK!!) Ask groups to circle those things that someone can change, then focus the discussion on the difference between criticism and picking on someone.

HOMEWORK: Write about a time you were criticized for something.

LESSON 44: CONSTRUCTIVE CRITICISM
UNIT: CRITICISM AND ATTITUDES

OBJECTIVE: To understand and demonstrate how to criticize in a constructive way.

Group Activity:

1. Define *constructive criticism* as criticizing someone's actions in a way that is positive and that helps the person find ways to improve.

2. Discuss the differences between constructive criticism and put-downs. Review the rules for giving criticism, pointing out the importance of criticizing someone's behavior, not the person.

ACTIVITY: Complete "Block the Attack" activity on the next page to practice recognizing constructive criticism vs. put-downs. Review when finished.

HOMEWORK: Have you ever been put down? Please explain. What could the person have said to you instead?

BLOCK THE ATTACK

GOOD CHARACTER

*DIRECTIONS: Read each of the statements below and decide if the statement is attacking or offering constructive criticism. Place an **A** on the line if it is a verbal attack on someone or **C** if it is constructive criticism.*

_____ 1. It might be helpful if you would read me the directions again.

_____ 2. How could you think that!

_____ 3. Have you ever seen anything so stupid in your life?

_____ 4. Maybe you should go back to the store and tell them they gave you the wrong change.

_____ 5. Why do you have to be such a jerk?

_____ 6. I think you would be happier with a different roommate.

_____ 7. Would you like me to help you practice hitting a fast ball?

_____ 8. Your dream vacation is to go to Nashville? Who's your cousin—Elvis?

_____ 9. It's probably not a good idea to stand under that tree while it's lightning.

_____ 10. I think you would look better if you colored your hair.

_____ 11. You have some pretty weird friends.

_____ 12. Why do you leave your clothes on the floor? You live like a slob.

_____ 13. All you do is complain; does anything make you happy?

_____ 14. If you spend some more time studying, your grades will improve.

_____ 15. I would appreciate it if you would come to class on time.

LESSON 45: COMMANDS OR SUGGESTIONS?
UNIT: CRITICISM AND ATTITUDES

OBJECTIVE: To understand the differences between commanding someone to do something and offering a suggestion.

Group Activity:

1. Discuss the differences between a command and a suggestion. Example: When we suggest things to do, it gives people a choice. They are more likely to change than if we dictate their actions.

2. Ask students what happens to communication and how others react to you when you make a command. Example: Sometimes we think we are making a suggestion, but we sound demanding. This can lead to a breakdown in communication. HINT: watch facial expressions!

ACTIVITY: Complete "Command or Suggestion?" activity on the next page and discuss the results when finished.

HOMEWORK: Write about a recent occasion when you thought you were making a suggestion and someone became offended. What happened? What could you have said differently?

COMMAND OR SUGGESTION?

DIRECTIONS: *Read the following commands and change them into suggestions on the line provided.*

1. Clean up your room.

   _____

2. Close that door, we're not heating the outdoors.

   _____

3. Just tell her that you want to go out with her.

   _____

4. Don't listen to him, I know what I'm talking about.

   _____

5. If it's busy, dial the other number.

   _____

6. It's cold outside, put on a sweater.

   _____

7. Bring those CDs to the party tonight.

   _____

8. Take your social studies book home tonight to study for the test.

   _____

9. Sit down!

   _____

10. Get here on time, I'm sick of your being late for everything.

   _____

LESSON 46: ACCEPTING CRITICISM
UNIT: CRITICISM AND ATTITUDES

OBJECTIVE: To recognize when someone is trying to give us criticism, and listen to the criticism without getting angry.

Group Activity:

1. Review the definition of *criticism* and discuss what it means to accept criticism.

    - Listen carefully without getting angry. (They are not picking on you, just trying to help.)

    - Try to learn from your mistakes.

    - Don't pick a fight, even if you feel that you are right.

2. Talk about what to do when responding to criticism.

    - Think about if the criticism is constructive or a put-down.

    - Who made the comment? (Authority, friends, etc.)

    - Think about how you should respond.

    - It is okay to ask the person to hear your side of the story, but you need to ask politely.

ACTIVITY: Pair students for role-playing. Ask them to choose one of the situations from the next page and practice accepting and giving criticism.

HOMEWORK: What is hard about accepting criticism for you? Please explain.

ACCEPTING CRITICISM ROLE PLAYS

DIRECTIONS: Choose one of the following situations and practice giving and accepting criticism.

1. Your best friend is ignoring you and says that you are being a snob. What will you say to him/her?

2. You just got a new hairstyle and your boyfriend/girlfriend told you that you should have never gotten it cut.

3. Your parents told you to be home by midnight because it is a school night. You are two hours late and they have been waiting up for you. When you come in, they tell you how irresponsible you are.

4. You drop your books going into school and everybody saw you. Your friends who are with you start to tell you how clumsy you are and ask if you need them to carry your books.

5. In the past, you have been known to stretch the truth with your parents. They ask you if there was drinking at a party you went to. Honestly, you told them no, but they tell you that you are not telling the truth again and that they cannot trust you.

6. You got into a fight with another kid at school. The principal sits you down in his office and tells you that you are acting like a punk.

LESSON 47: COMMUNICATION BREAKDOWN
UNIT: CRITICISM AND ATTITUDES

OBJECTIVE: To help students recognize how they communicate when being criticized and to understand how their reactions might block communication.

Group Activity:

1. Discuss the importance of good communication skills when accepting and giving criticism. Our reactions to criticism are equally as important as what is being said to us.

2. As a group, go over each of the obstacles to good communication on the next page.

ACTIVITY: Ask students to complete the questionnaire about their communication skills when they are being criticized. Review when finished.

HOMEWORK: Which of the obstacles to good communication have you used? Choose no more than four and discuss why you use those obstacles.

OBSTACLES TO GOOD COMMUNICATION

1. **Name-calling:** No one likes to admit that they are wrong, but calling others names because we are embarrassed or angry can stop the other person from listening.

2. **Translating:** When someone criticizes us for something, it is not our place to add our own thoughts and blow the message out of proportion. Ask the person to clear up the criticism if you don't understand.

3. **Generalizing:** When giving criticism, avoid terms such as: "You always" or "You never" because it is accusatory and when one thing happens, it doesn't mean it always or never will.

4. **Gossiping:** Just because we don't like to hear criticism sometimes, we should not seek revenge on the person giving the criticism by talking behind his/her back. Spreading rumors is inappropriate.

5. **Explanations:** Try not to use too many words when giving criticism. We should not outline every thing the person did to upset us. Get to the point, then let the other person talk. Too much explaining will tune the other person out.

6. **Blaming:** Even if you think the other person is wrong, we should criticize his/her actions, not the person. Blaming others for our mistakes does not allow for clear communication. Accept responsibility.

7. **Shouting:** When criticizing others, remember that they have feelings too. No one likes to be yelled at and you will get your point across more effectively if you talk to the person and not demean him/her.

8. **Badgering:** Once you have had your say and criticized the actions of the other person, give them time to change. If we constantly remind the person of his/her mistakes, he/she may start to resent you. Try to be patient.

CRITICIZE BUT COMMUNICATE

DIRECTIONS: Think about the obstacles to communication you use when being criticized or giving criticism to others. Read each of the questions below and rate your criticism communication skills.

KEY: A = always · S = sometimes · N = never

_____ 1. When I give others criticism, I sound bossy by telling them what to do.

_____ 2. I make up a story about the person who criticized me.

_____ 3. I often think the person who is giving me criticism is wrong.

_____ 4. I listen to the person when they are giving me criticism.

_____ 5. I ask questions of the person giving me criticism.

_____ 6. When answering someone's criticism, I use the terms "You never" or "You always."

_____ 7. I feel defensive when someone gives me criticism.

_____ 8. I badmouth people who give me criticism.

_____ 9. When someone gives me criticism, I genuinely try to change.

_____ 10. When I give criticism, I also give suggestions to the person.

_____ 11. I criticize behaviors, not the person.

_____ 12. I listen to my friends' criticism more than the criticism from my parents.

_____ 13. When I criticize, I tend to detail everything the person did wrong.

_____ 14. I can easily admit when I am wrong.

_____ 15. I mistake anger for embarrassment and tend to yell when criticized.

LESSON 48: DEFENSE MECHANISMS
UNIT: CRITICISM AND ATTITUDES

OBJECTIVE: To help students identify and evaluate defense mechanisms and recognize which defense mechanisms they use.

Group Activity:

1. Define the term *defense mechanism*. Defense mechanisms are tools we use to cope and protect ourselves from the anxiety caused in various situations.

2. Discuss the defense mechanisms on the next page and be sure students understand each. Give examples when necessary.

ACTIVITY: Complete "Defense Mechanisms: Friend or Foe?" activity and review when finished.

HOMEWORK: Which defense mechanisms do you use most often? Explain why you think these are the ones you use.

DEFENSE MECHANISMS

1. **Making Excuses:** Fooling yourself into believing that something isn't as bad as it seems. Rationalizing. Making an excuse to make something seem right.

2. **Concealing:** Purposely forgetting something that is hard to cope with. Repressing a hurtful thought or memory.

3. **Ignoring the Truth:** Denying that something is happening. Believing that something is not true and not admitting to the truth.

4. **Opposite Reaction:** Acting in a way that is the opposite of your real feelings because the real feelings are too painful.

5. **Relapsing:** Acting immature. Not acting your age in order to get attention or to try to get out of dealing with the pain. Acting like a baby.

6. **Fantasy:** Imagining that things will be better than they possibly could be. Escaping from coping with a situation by daydreaming.

7. **Casting:** Blaming others for unacceptable or painful feelings. Accusing others for making us feel the way we do.

8. **Substituting:** Taking our feelings out on others when they did not cause the feelings in the first place. Displacing the pain or anger.

9. **Changing the Subject:** Talking about something other than how we feel in order to avoid dealing with the pain.

DEFENSE MECHANISMS: FRIEND OR FOE?

DIRECTIONS: Read each of the situations below and write which defense mechanism is being used on the line provided.

1. You didn't make the volleyball team. When your mother asks you how try-outs went, you yell at her to leave you alone.

   _____

   _____

2. You found out that your boyfriend/girlfriend likes your best friend but you still are as nice as ever to both of them.

   _____

   _____

3. You come home in a bad mood and tell your sister to stop being such a grump.

   _____

   _____

4. You aren't cast in the lead role in the school play, but you are in the costume department. All through the production, you say that it is a stupid play and you really didn't want to have a part in it.

   _____

   _____

5. You can't remember the college that rejected your application.

_____

_____

6. You think that you will be selected to play in the Boston Symphony Orchestra someday because you are the best cellist in the school.

_____

_____

7. You began smoking at a young age and you tell everyone that you can quit anytime you want.

_____

_____

8. You were rejected for a date with the most popular person in school and begin to call him/her names and tease him/her.

_____

_____

9. A friend begins to talk to you about the test you both failed, but you ignore him and talk about what to do over the weekend.

LESSON 49: SELF-CRITICISM
UNIT: CRITICISM AND ATTITUDES

OBJECTIVE: To understand the positive and negative aspects of criticizing ourselves.

Group Activity:

1. Review the definition of *criticism* if necessary.

2. Discuss criticizing ourselves. Emphasize that we can be both positive and negative when criticizing the things that we do. Our minds believe the things we tell it and we tend to be harder on ourselves than on others.

ACTIVITY: Complete "Talking to Yourself" activity and discuss the results when finished.

HOMEWORK: How hard are you on yourself? Explain the last time you criticized yourself for something.

TALKING TO YOURSELF

DIRECTIONS: For each of the situations below, write what you would tell yourself. Make one positive and one negative statement about the situation.

SITUATION	POSITIVE	NEGATIVE
You were invited to a party and your parents won't let you go. You sneak out and get caught.		
You studied all night for the big math exam. When you handed in the test, you knew you aced it. When you got the test back, you only got a C.		
You tried out for the varsity basketball team and did not make it. This means one more year on J.V.		
You just found out that your parents are getting a divorce and when you try to help, they tell you to stay out of it.		
You've had your eye on the most popular kid in the school and there is a school dance this Friday night. You're a little nervous about asking for a date.		
You're afraid to join the year book club in school because it's not what the cool kids do.		
Your best friend bought some alcohol from another student and asks you to drink with him but you don't want to drink.		

LESSON 50: FAILURE AND SUCCESS
UNIT: CRITICISM AND ATTITUDES

OBJECTIVE: To help students understand that failure is a part of everyday life and to understand how our attitudes can help us change failures into successes.

Group Activity:

1. Define *attitude* as the way we see things. Talk about the importance of having a positive attitude about the things we do.

2. Brainstorm the different things we do that may lead to failure.
   - Trying new things.
   - Not listening and following directions.
   - Not having the opportunities that others have.

3. Talk about the variety of things people can do to help improve their attitudes and overcome failure. Giving up is NOT an option!
   - Ask for help even if it isn't cool to do so.
   - Take criticism as a positive way to help you.
   - Do things in steps: little successes build up self-esteem.

ACTIVITY: Students fill out strengths and weaknesses questionnaire on the next page in order to assess areas in which they feel they may fail.

HOMEWORK: Write about a time you failed at something, but did not give up. Explain why you chose to keep trying.

CHANGING FAILURE INTO SUCCESS

DIRECTIONS: Answer the following questions. Be sure to be honest in your answers so you can see where you need to change your attitude.

1. What activities scare you? What are the things you are afraid to try?

2. What is it about the above activities that makes you afraid?

3. What do you feel the most proud about? What is your greatest accomplishment?

4. Have you ever felt so frustrated about something that you just wanted to give up? If so, what was it and what frustrated you?

5. In your opinion, how can failure be a positive experience?

6. Everyone has failed at something in their lives. What do you tell yourself when you fail at something?

7. What are the things you would like to improve upon and why?

8. List the things you can do to improve the above things.

CRITICISM
QUOTATIONS OF THE WEEK:

*"Sticks and stones may break our bones,
but words will break our hearts. "*
- Robert Fulghum -

*"A man should never be ashamed to own that he has been
in the wrong, which is but saying, that he is wiser today
than he was yesterday."*
- Jonathan Swift -

"No one can make you feel inferior without your consent."
- Eleanor Roosevelt -

*"Have patience with all things,
but chiefly have patience with yourself.
Do not lose courage in considering your own imperfections,
but instantly set about remedying them..."*
- St. Francis de Sales -

"There is no failure except in no longer trying."
- Kin Hubbard -

*"The greatest revolution in our generation is
the discovery that human beings, by changing
the inner attitudes of their minds
can change the outer aspects of their lives."*
- William James -

Teacher tip:
Pin one of the quotations to a bulletin board
and ask students to reflect on what is said,
apply it to their thinking and explain if they
agree with it. You may have them write
about it in their value journals.

STRESS MANAGEMENT

Stress management is important to anyone who wants to live a socially productive life. Stress is often unavoidable and stress-management skills are sometimes difficult. In this unit, students learn what stress is and what kinds of events cause stress. Students will be able to recognize stressful situations as well as their stress thresholds. Students will be able to recognize the different emotions they feel and how to manage those emotions. The unit also contains exercises to help students realize when they are having impractical thoughts, how to recognize and manage their anger, and how to maintain self-control in various situations.

LESSON 51: STRESS AND STRESSORS
UNIT: STRESS MANAGEMENT

OBJECTIVE: To recognize and understand what stress is and what causes stressful feelings.

Group Activity:

1. Define *stress* as anything that produces physical or mental strain. Define *stressors* as the things that cause stress.

2. Brainstorm both positive and negative stressors. Be sure to discuss each stressor on the list.

   - Playing in a big game.
   - Too much homework.
   - Too many expectations.

ACTIVITY: Divide students into groups of two or three. Distribute poster board to each group and ask them to make "Stressor Collages." Ask groups to cut pictures and phrases out of magazines or draw objects to represent stressors. They may want to separate the positives and the negatives.

HOMEWORK: Write about the things that stress you out—both positive and negative. Describe at least four stressors in your life.

LESSON 52: STRESSFUL SITUATIONS
UNIT: STRESS MANAGEMENT

OBJECTIVE: To learn to recognize stressful situations and determine a way to deal with stress.

Group Activity:

1. Explain that there are different categories of stressful situations. Describe each one and give examples where needed.

2. Stress categories:

   - Predictable: You know what will happen and you can avoid it.

   - Unavoidable: You know what will happen, but you can't escape.

   - Unaware: You don't know what is coming and you cannot avoid it.

ACTIVITY: Ask students to complete the "Categories of Stress" activity on the next page. You may choose to do this activity together or independently.

HOMEWORK: Write out your personal list of stressors and place them into the appropriate categories of stressful situations.

CATEGORIES OF STRESS

DIRECTIONS: Read each of the following situations and place them under the appropriate stress category.

Don't forget to ask yourself: Do I have a choice or is this situation something I can't get out of? Is this something I can see coming?

Hitchhiking	**A Blind Date**	**Someone Not Listening**
Finals	**Working Late**	**Too Much Homework**
Acne	**Strep Throat**	**Being Rejected for a Date**
Mean Teachers	**Team Tryouts**	**Unprotected Sex**
Car Accident	**Parents' Divorce**	**Pleasing Your Friends**
Keeping up with Trends	**Smoking**	**Death of a Friend**

PREDICTABLE	UNAVOIDABLE	UNAWARE

LESSON 53: SIGNS OF STRESS
UNIT: STRESS MANAGEMENT

OBJECTIVE: To recognize the physical and the emotional signs of stress and understand the different reactions people have to stress.

Group Activity:

1. Review the definitions of stress and stressors.

2. Brainstorm and discuss the signs of stress.

   - Physical: sweating, headaches, stomachaches, heart races
   - Emotional: crying, anxiety, yelling, etc.

3. Discuss the reactions people have to stress.

   - Losing interest in things that were enjoyable.
   - Arguing with anyone.
   - Alcohol/drug abuse.
   - Hiding from reality.

ACTIVITY: Complete "Am I Stressed Out?!" activity on the next page and discuss when finished.

HOMEWORK: What happens to you when you are stressed out? Talk about both the physical and emotional reactions you have.

AM I STRESSED OUT?!

DIRECTIONS: Read each of the following situations and decide if the person should feel stressed out. If so, indicate why on the line provided. If not, just state no.

1. It is the end of the school year and finals are coming up. As you are studying, your sister comes into your room and asks if you want to go out for ice cream. You say, "Can't you just leave me alone?!"

   _____

   _____

2. It's your only free Saturday this month and you have to go to a family reunion in the afternoon, but your best friend invited you up to their camp. You friend needs to know if you're coming.

   _____

   _____

3. It's the day of a big soccer game and you are scheduled to start. Your math teacher told you to stay after school to make up a test you failed.

   _____

   _____

4. It's the day of graduation and you were invited to three different graduation parties.

   _____

   _____

5. Lately, your parents have been fighting about anything and every- thing. They tell you that everything is okay, but you don't think so.

_____

_____

6. You are a writer for the school paper and the editor has been criticizing your work quite a bit lately. Instead of talking to the editor, you decide to work on the next story through the weekend.

_____

_____

7. Your friend got tickets to the concert you've been wanting to see, but your parents tell you that you can't go until you finish the housework.

_____

_____

LESSON 54: WAYS TO HANDLE STRESS
UNIT: STRESS MANAGEMENT

OBJECTIVE: To help students understand and practice different techniques that can be used to deal with stressful situations.

Group Activity:

1. Review the various signs that appear when we are feeling stress.

2. Discuss the different ways people deal with stressful situations. Brainstorm others.

   - Deep breathing.
   - Exercise: walking, biking.
   - Talking to someone you trust.
   - Spending some time alone.

ACTIVITY: Divide the class into small groups and distribute situation cards. Ask each group to list the signs that show the person on their card is under stress. What is causing the person to feel like he/she is losing control? What can he/she do to manage the stress? Each group reports after completed.

HOMEWORK: Write about a time when you felt really stressed out. How did you manage the stress? Please explain.

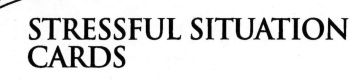

STRESSFUL SITUATION CARDS

DIRECTIONS: Choose one of the situations below and discuss how you know the person is stressed out, what is causing the stress and how he/she should handle it.

You've been asked out on a date with one of the most popular people in the school. Rumor has it that this person is only going out with you because his/her friends dared him/her to. You want to confront the person but you can feel your heart racing and you are sweating.

Your friends are going to a new club that opened up, but your parents told you that you couldn't go until the weekend. Everyone will be there tonight, so you sneak out of the house. You aren't really having a good time because you're afraid you'll get caught.

Your teachers have moved you up to more advanced level classes. This means not only more work, but you won't see your friends as much. This type of work could help you in the future and that is important to your parents. Your first night of homework took you four hours to finish. You ask, "Is it worth all this? Will I disappoint everyone?"

The person you have been dating for about six months decides that it is time for you to "go all the way." You are not ready to have sex with this person but you are afraid that if you don't, he/she will break up with you.

LESSON 55: RECOGNIZING EMOTIONS
UNIT: STRESS MANAGEMENT

OBJECTIVE: To help students recognize the different emotions that people feel and understand the events that trigger a certain emotion.

Group Activity:

1. Define *emotions* as a state of feeling or the way we feel about something or someone.

2. Brainstorm different emotions. Get a working list of emotions and compare with the list on the next page.

ACTIVITY: Review the emotions list on the next page. Provide definitions and offer examples when necessary.

HOMEWORK: List the emotions you feel most often and explain what makes you feel each emotion.

EMOTIONAL NOTIONS

ANGER	FEAR	DISAPPOINTED
AGGRAVATED	ENERGETIC	GUILTY
ALIENATED	CONFIDENT	JEALOUS
RELIEVED	FRUSTRATED	CONFUSED
LONELY	PARANOID	PROUD
SHY	ANXIOUS	HOSTILE
BORED	DEPRESSED	HURT
EMBARRASSED	SAD	HAPPY
SURPRISED	HELPLESS	LOVED
DISCOURAGED	HUMILIATED	REGRETFUL

LESSON 56: SIGNS OF EMOTIONAL STRESS
UNIT: STRESS MANAGEMENT

OBJECTIVE: To help students recognize the signs of various kinds of emotional stress and to interpret the signs accurately.

Group Activity:

1. Review the emotions sheet and insure that all the students understand the emotions.

2. Discuss the physical effects people feel when they are under emotional stress—both positive and negative.

3. Make comparison lists of emotions that are commonly mistaken.

   - Frustration mistaken for anger.
   - Jealousy mistaken for anger.
   - Anxiousness mistaken for fear.
   - Worry mistaken for sadness.

ACTIVITY: Complete "Emotions in Motion" activity on the next page. Discuss the results when finished.

HOMEWORK: Write about a time when you felt one emotion, but others thought you were feeling something else.

The Power of Social Skills in Character Development | **Stress Management**

EMOTIONS IN MOTION

DIRECTIONS: Read each of the following situations and identify the proper emotion(s) on the line provided.

1. You and your friend are going to a party and neither one of you knows anybody at the party. How would you feel?

    _____

    _____

2. The prom is coming up and you have to go shopping. You've made a list, but you feel like you are forgetting something.

    _____

    _____

3. Three of your friends are outside talking and when you approach them, they stop and just look at you.

    _____

    _____

4. You've been chosen to run for student government president.

    _____

    _____

5. You are a vegetarian and the person you are dating likes to hunt.

    _____

    _____

6. You are waiting for your boyfriend/girlfriend to pick you up for your date and he/she stands you up.

_____

_____

7. That killer history exam is handed back corrected and you aced it.

_____

_____

8. There is only one more position on the swim team and you are trying out for it.

_____

_____

9. You just looked at the schedule at work and realized that this is the fourth weekend in a row that you are scheduled.

_____

_____

10. Your best friend of ten years just told you that he is moving away.

_____

_____

LESSON 57: STRESS THRESHOLD
UNIT: STRESS MANAGEMENT

OBJECTIVE: To help students recognize their stress level and to identify their limit before they lose control.

Group Activity:

1. Define a *threshold* as a level or point that we determine as a limit.

2. Discuss the things that bring us up to our emotional threshold and possibly push us over the edge.

ACTIVITY: Complete "Stress Threshold Survey" on the next page and discuss the results when finished.

HOMEWORK: Do you feel like you have a lot of stress in your life? Does this stress make you feel emotional and if so, in what ways?

STRESS THRESHOLD SURVEY

DIRECTIONS: Take the following quiz to determine your stress threshold. When finished answering the questions, add up the circled numbers and check the Stress-O-Meter.

1 = Never · 2 = Hardly · 3 = Sometimes · 4 = Often · 5 = Always

1.	I speak rather quickly.	1	2	3	4	5
2.	I interrupt others and try to finish their sentences.	1	2	3	4	5
3.	I have a hard time finishing things I am supposed to do.	1	2	3	4	5
4.	I eat fast and sometimes I eat standing up.	1	2	3	4	5
5.	I take on more than one thing at a time.	1	2	3	4	5
6.	I don't have much down-time or time to myself.	1	2	3	4	5
7.	I get impatient when others walk or drive too slow.	1	2	3	4	5
8.	I think about other things when people are talking to me.	1	2	3	4	5
9.	I am a competitive person.	1	2	3	4	5
10.	I tap my fingers and wiggle my feet a lot.	1	2	3	4	5
11.	It is hard for me to be alone.	1	2	3	4	5
12.	I keep a calendar or appointment book.	1	2	3	4	5
13.	When I get upset, I yell or throw things.	1	2	3	4	5
14.	I walk quickly.	1	2	3	4	5
15.	I feel like I don't have enough time to get everything done.	1	2	3	4	5

Stress-O-Meter:

10 – 50: You deal with Stress Well

55 – 70: Work on Your Management Techniques

70 + : Stressed Out!

LESSON 58: IMPRACTICAL THOUGHTS
UNIT: STRESS MANAGEMENT

OBJECTIVE: To recognize when we are thinking irrationally and how to change thinking patterns to help reduce stress.

Group Activity:

1. Define *impractical* as not being logical or not making sense.

2. Discuss the different types of impractical thoughts that can lead us to add stress to our lives.

   - Overgeneralizing.
   - Jumping to conclusions.
   - Exaggerating.
   - Accentuating the negative.
   - Taking statements personally.

3. Brainstorm things we can do to overcome impractical thoughts.

   - Live in the present, don't dwell on the past.
   - Let go of bad relationships.
   - Believe in yourself!
   - Check out all the facts BEFORE you judge others.

ACTIVITY: Complete "Calculated Thoughts" activity and discuss the results when finished.

HOMEWORK: What are the types of things you think impractical thoughts about? How can you personally change your way of thinking?

CALCULATED THOUGHTS

DIRECTIONS: Read each of the following situations and write one impractical thought and one logical thought in the box provided.

SITUATION	IMPRACTICAL	LOGICAL
Your friend is two hours late to meet you.		
You've gone out on a couple of dates with someone you really like, but he/she hasn't called you in a week.		
The CD you want is on sale, but when you get to the store there is only one copy left. As you looked at something else, someone took the last copy.		
You were picked to play on the volleyball team, but you have never played on a team before.		
You are late for class and as you rush toward the room, you run into one of your teachers and she falls on the floor.		
You've written a short story in English class and your friend tells you to enter it in a contest in your favorite magazine.		

LESSON 59: RECOGNIZING ANGER
UNIT: STRESS MANAGEMENT

OBJECTIVE:

To understand what anger is and where it comes from, as well as to notice situations that may cause angry feelings.

Group Activity:

1. Define *anger* as an emotional feeling of displeasure that can cause problems and feelings of rage.

2. Discuss how body language and how we carry ourselves can show anger. Point out that some people may look angry, but aren't. This can affect how others react and feel about you.

ACTIVITY:

Distribute colored paper or poster board to each student and ask them to create an anger acronym. For each letter in the word ANGER, have students think of characteristics that are related to anger. For example:

A = aggressive, anxious, annoyed, alone, awful

HOMEWORK:

How can anger produce stress and cause problems for you? How do you feel when you are angry?

LESSON 60: REACTIONS TO ANGER
UNIT: STRESS MANAGEMENT

OBJECTIVE: To notice when anger is building inside us and to understand the positive and negative ways to react to anger.

Group Activity:

1. Brainstorm the different ways people react to things when they are angry.
   - Yell.
   - Throw things.
   - Hit or punch.

2. Discuss the positive ways we can react when we are angry.
   - Talk to someone who is a good listener.
   - Avoid watching violence on TV
   - Keep a journal.

ACTIVITY: Complete "Reaction Formation" activity to see how students view anger as well as how they react to it.

HOMEWORK: How do you usually deal with anger? Would you like to change your reactions? Please explain why.

REACTION FORMATION

DIRECTIONS: Read the following statements about anger to see how you react and what you think about angry feelings. Place the appropriate number on the line provided.

1 = Strongly Agree · 2 = Agree · 3 = Undecided
4 = Disagree · 5 = Strongly Disagree

_____ 1. I get angry at others easily.

_____ 2. I am a shouter; I yell when I am angry.

_____ 3. I often smile throughout the day.

_____ 4. I feel pressured and under stress often.

_____ 5. I get upset when someone yells at me.

_____ 6. I sometimes throw things when I am angry.

_____ 7. I withdraw or don't talk to anyone when I am angry.

_____ 8. I hold everything inside.

_____ 9. People should not express their anger, they should just deal with it.

_____ 10. How I react when I am mad really shows how I feel about myself.

_____ 11. Sometimes I act nice, but I am furious inside.

_____ 12. I have gotten so mad that I've made myself sick.

_____ 13. I get mad at myself often.

_____ 14. I become angry easily.

_____ 15. I sometimes mistake anger for other emotions.

LESSON 61: REGAINING SELF-CONTROL
UNIT: STRESS MANAGEMENT

OBJECTIVE: To help students learn strategies they can use to regain self-control when they are angry.

Group Activity:

1. Review the definition for anger. Define *self-control* as keeping a hold over your emotions or impulses.

2. Discuss the steps students can use to control their anger. This may help when they cannot walk away from the situation.

   - Stop what you are doing.
   - Take a deep breath, count to 10, etc.
   - Identify the true feelings: guilt, anger, fear, embarrassed.
   - Think about what made you feel this way. (It may not be someone else's fault.)
   - Talk to someone about the situation.

3. The above things may be applied when we can leave the situation. Emphasize that it is important to get out all the built-up energy BEFORE trying to regain self-control. We all think clearer once we calm down.

   - Go for a walk.
   - Punch a pillow.
   - Have a good cry.

ACTIVITY: Pair students for role-playing. Ask them to choose one of the situations on the next page and practice regaining self-control.

HOMEWORK: What do you do (or what will you now do) to regain your self-control when you are angry? Explain why.

The Power of Social Skills in Character Development | **Stress Management**

SELF-CONTROL ROLE-PLAYS

GOOD CHARACTER

DIRECTIONS: Choose one of the following situations. Try to choose one that you have experienced and practice regaining self-control. Remember, as you reflect on when the situation happened, you may become angry.

1. Your social studies teacher seems to grade your papers more harshly than he grades anyone else's paper.

2. You were bumped off the basketball team because you missed two practices in a row. These practices were missed because you needed to get extra help in math.

3. You were with a friend in a record store. Your friend stole a CD and both of you were accused of stealing.

4. Your brother promised to take you to the mall today, but he already left the house for the day.

5. Your boyfriend/girlfriend of six months broke up with you to go out with someone else.

6. You finally have your driver's license and you've saved up all your money for a car. You found the perfect one, but your parents tell you that you can't buy it now.

7. The kid who sits next to you in Spanish class keeps cheating off of you. You've told him to stop, but he won't.

STRESS MANAGEMENT
QUOTATIONS OF THE WEEK:

"You gain strength,courage and confidence by every experience
in which you really stop to look fear in the face...
you must do the thing you think you cannot do."
- Eleanor Roosevelt -

"If you want to lift yourself up, lift up someone else."
- Booker T. Washington -

"On every level of life from housework to heights of prayer,
in all judgement and all efforts to get things done,
hurry and impatience are sure marks of the amateur."
- Evelyn Underhill -

"Never stop. One always stops as something
is about to happen."
- Peter Brook -

"Slow and steady wins the race."
- Aesop, The Hare and the Tortise -

"Before you give up hope, turn back and read the attacks
that were made upon Lincoln"
- Bruce Barton -

Teacher tip:
Pin one of the quotations above to a bulletin
board and ask students to reflect on what is
said, apply it to their thinking and explain if
they agree with it. You may have them write
about in their value journals.

CONFLICT RESOLUTION AND PROBLEM SOLVING

In this unit, students learn to recognize a conflict, understand what causes conflicts, and develop tactics to cope with conflicts in their lives. They will recognize that there are situations when conflicts cannot be avoided and will learn how to deal with those situations when they arise. Students will understand the basic psychological needs people have and how bias and stereotyping can make their way into our thinking. Students will learn resolution techniques: how to recognize a problem, how to develop problem-solving strategies, and when to be passive or assertive. Students will realize the importance of taking responsibility for their actions and the need for patience and perseverance in resolving conflicts peacefully.

LESSON 62: RECOGNIZING CONFLICTS
UNIT: CONFLICT RESOLUTION
AND PROBLEM SOLVING

OBJECTIVE: To help students recognize when a conflict is beginning and understand the characteristics of conflicts.

Group Activity:

1. Define *conflict* as a difference in point of view that may lead to a fight or battle.

2. Brainstorm characteristics of a conflict.

   • Disagreements.

   • Hurt feelings.

   • Feelings of anger.

   • Saying or doing regrettable things.

ACTIVITY: In-class journal: Write about a conflict you are having with someone right now. What is it about and how did it start? Discuss the different characteristics of the students' conflicts and keep a list of them to hang up in the classroom.

HOMEWORK: Have you ever started a conflict with someone? If so, what did you do or say to start the fight? Please explain.

LESSON 63: CAUSES OF CONFLICT
UNIT: CONFLICT RESOLUTION
AND PROBLEM SOLVING

OBJECTIVE: To understand the four basic human psychological needs and how these needs are at the base of most conflicts.

Group Activity:

Define and discuss the four basic psychological needs:

- *Relationship:* belonging to a group and developing a bond in order to show love, cooperation, and caring.

- *Capability:* having the power to set goals, accomplish, and be recognized for hard work.

- *Independence:* making our own choices and decisions.

- *Pleasure:* entertaining ourselves, laughing, and enjoying our lives.

ACTIVITY: Use the "Needs Assessment" on the next page and ask students to list their basic psychological needs in the boxes provided.

HOMEWORK: Using your basic psychological needs assessment, why are these the things you chose in your life? Please explain.

NEEDS ASSESSMENT

DIRECTIONS: In the boxes provided, list the things in your life that fit under each basic needs category.

RELATIONSHIP	INDEPENDENCE

CAPABILITY	PLEASURE

LESSON 64: BASIC PSYCHOLOGICAL NEEDS APPLICATION
UNIT: CONFLICT RESOLUTION AND PROBLEM SOLVING

OBJECTIVE: To better understand the four basic psychological needs and practice identifying them.

Group Activity:

1. Review the basic psychological needs and answer any questions.

2. Discuss that when our basic psychological needs are not met or when our value base is violated, conflicts occur.

ACTIVITY: Complete "Basic Psychological Needs Identification" activity on the next page. Discuss the results when finished.

HOMEWORK: Take your conflict and basic psychological needs lists and make a chart of the things you have conflicts about and place them under the proper need category.

BASIC PSYCHOLOGICAL NEEDS IDENTIFICATION

DIRECTIONS: Read each of the situations below. They may be future conflicts. Identify in the box provided which basic psychological need is unmet in each situation.

1. Your friend is going to a party and you were not invited.

2. Your family saved up some money. Your mother wants to go on vacation, but your father wants a new car.

3. You are speaking to a friend and another friend continues to interrupt you and tries to finish your sentences.

4. Your sister is allowed to stay out until midnight, but you have to be in by 10:00 P.M. You voice your opinion to your parents, but they don't want to listen.

5. One person applies for the same job as his friend.

6. Everyone was planing to go to the beach this afternoon but no one called you to tell you what time.

7. Your boyfriend's best friend for years is female and he tells her things he won't tell you.

8. You have a feeling that your brother has been using your stereo and borrowing your CDs.

9. Your parents have planned to move, but they told you that you could finish out the school year with your friends. You came home from school and found out that the family is moving six months early.

LESSON 65: BIAS AND STEREOTYPE IDENTIFICATION
UNIT: CONFLICT RESOLUTION AND PROBLEM SOLVING

OBJECTIVE: To help students understand the difference between biases and stereotypes, as well as to recognize their own biases.

Group Activity:

1. Define *bias* as a certain feeling we have about something or someone that may be prejudiced.

2. Define *stereotype* as a picture in our heads we have of something or someone without knowing about it.

3. Discuss the general stereotypes and biases we may hold without realizing they are such.

   - Girls are smarter than boys.
   - All Germans have blond hair and blue eyes.
   - Men are stronger than women.

   Continue to discuss how these views can begin a conflict.

ACTIVITY: Distribute "Are You Ripe for Conflict?" questionnaire on the next page. Students evaluate their own biases and feelings toward others. Discuss the results when finished.

HOMEWORK: What are your biases and stereotypical feelings? Why do you have them. Have you ever acted on them toward anyone else? Please explain.

ARE YOU RIPE FOR CONFLICT?

DIRECTIONS: Read each of the questions below and answer them as honestly as possible. Keep in mind that feeling a certain way does not make you a bad person, just more aware of yourself.

Y = yes, I feel this way
N = no, I don't feel this way
S = sometimes I feel this way

_____ 1. Both men and women should be equal.

_____ 2. I stare at people with physical handicaps.

_____ 3. I would not date someone of a different race than me.

_____ 4. I make generalizations about others such as: "fat people are lazy and shouldn't eat so much."

_____ 5. If in a dating situation, one person says no, he/she really means yes.

_____ 6. There should be no discrimination toward anyone.

_____ 7. If a friend was making fun of someone else, I would try to stop the teasing.

_____ 8. People really can't change their situations and might as well accept the fact that they are different.

_____ 9. It is good to express our own individuality.

_____ 10. There is a lot of diversity in my relationships. I like to know about others' different customs and practices.

GOOD CHARACTER

LESSON 66: FIGHTING FAIR
UNIT: CONFLICT RESOLUTION AND PROBLEM SOLVING

OBJECTIVE: To understand that conflicts are a part of life and to learn how to fight fair (verbally) when the conflict cannot be avoided.

Group Activity:

1. Explain that conflicts occur over both small and large things in our lives. There are ways to handle your conflict in a fair and respectful way. Our relationships can improve through conflict.

2. Go through the respectable practices in conflicts (below) and provide examples where needed.

   - Don't bring up things that don't have anything to do with the fight.
   - Avoid communication breakdown—keep talking.
   - Use "I" statements—don't attack!
   - Be honest and remember that this is someone you care about.
   - Don't blame; think before you speak.
   - Confrontations should be at the right time.

ACTIVITY: Complete "Is this a Fair Fight?" activity on the next page. Discuss the results when finished.

HOMEWORK: Do you think you fight fair? If not, how do you think you can improve your conflict resolution skills?

IS THIS A FAIR FIGHT?

DIRECTIONS: Read each of the situations below and tell if the people involved are fighting fair. If not, correct it on the line provided. If they are fighting fair, just write yes.

1. Janice came home from school where she failed a math test. Her mother wants to finish the argument that they started this morning. Janice yells at her mother telling her how stupid she is and can't she understand that it was a bad day?

   _____

2. Your boyfriend/girlfriend is 30 minutes late for your date. When he/she finally shows up, you accuse him/her of being with someone else and break up with him/her then walk away, not allowing the other person to explain.

   _____

3. Tim never voices his opinion to his girlfriend. She has been spending less and less time with him and he is beginning to wonder about their relationship. She accuses Tim of being insensitive to her feelings and he finally explodes to her with everything that has been bothering him about their relationship.

   _____

4. John gets home from work and tells Clarissa that he is really upset with something she said this morning. Clarissa asks if they can talk about it after dinner when they both have had time to clear their thoughts.

   _____

5. Sue feels that her boyfriend is not very affectionate and she asks him if he could hold her hand a little more often and say caring things to her sometimes.

   _____

6. James was angry at Joe about asking out a girl he had his eye on. James confronts Joe about the situation and Joe says, "Well, maybe you shouldn't have pointed her out to me." James punches Joe out and threatens him with more.

   _____

7. Your father has been very busy lately and has not spent much time with you. He wants to take you to a ball game on the one night you have plans. You change your plans because you aren't sure of the next time he will spend time with you.

   _____

LESSON 67: PASSIVE, AGGRESSIVE, ASSERTIVE

UNIT: CONFLICT RESOLUTION AND PROBLEM SOLVING

OBJECTIVE: To recognize the difference between passive, aggressive and assertive behavior and how these behaviors can affect not only self-esteem, but also how we deal with conflict.

Group Activity:

1. Define *passive*, *aggressive* and *assertive* and give examples of each.

   - *Passive:* not saying how you feel, allowing others to walk all over you.

   - *Aggressive:* demanding that people treat you with respect, while you don't show respect to others.

   - *Assertive:* standing up for yourself, but showing respect to others.

ACTIVITY: Complete the activity on recognizing passive, aggressive and assertive behavior on the next page. Discuss the results when finished.

HOMEWORK: Do you feel that your response to conflicts with others is passive, aggressive or assertive? Please explain. (Some of us feel a little of all three.)

PASSIVE, AGGRESSIVE OR ASSERTIVE?

DIRECTIONS: For each of the situations below, indicate on the line if the response is passive, aggressive or assertive.

1. Your boyfriend/girlfriend seems to pick on you for every little thing lately, but you don't say anything. He/she is just trying to help.

   _____

2. Your best friend tells you the great news, he was chosen to write for the school paper. It was the job you applied for and you tell him that if he was a true friend, he would not take the job.

   _____

3. You are trying to explain to your parents why you were late, but they keep interrupting you and each other, so you just talk louder.

   _____

4. There is a big party tonight and all of your homework is done, but your mother still won't let you go. You ask, "I don't understand why I can't go to the party if all my work is done."

   _____

5. Everyone knows you are a brain. One of your classmates approaches you and tells you to write his paper for him or he'll beat you up. You write the paper without saying a word.

   _____

6. You see someone steal a CD from the record store, but you just walk out. Why should you get involved?

   _____

7. Your French teacher keeps calling on you when you don't know the answers, so you say in your best French accent, "I don't know, why not ask someone else?"

   _____

8. While you are buying a pair of jeans, the cashier doesn't give you back the right change, so you accuse her of trying to rip you off.

   _____

LESSON 68: CONFLICT RESOLUTION
UNIT: CONFLICT RESOLUTION AND PROBLEM SOLVING

OBJECTIVE: To practice resolving conflicts in a peaceful and mature manner without attacking the other person.

Group Activity:

1. Review causes of conflicts as well as basic psychological needs.

2. Discuss steps to resolving conflicts.
   - Make sure your emotions are under control.
   - Identify the source of the conflict. (Don't accuse!)
   - Talk about how you feel and be sure to listen to the other person.
   - Make sure you understand each other.
   - Compromise and work together to find a solution. (Come up with as many things to do about the situation as possible.)
   - Ask for help if needed: teacher, peer mediator, etc.

3. Read the following situation and as a class resolve the conflict.

   Gene has been working out all summer in preparation for soccer team try-outs. He gets cut from the team and begs the coach for another try. The coach says no because there is not enough time.

ACTIVITY: Pair students for role-playing. Ask them to choose one of the situations on the next page and practice their conflict resolution techniques. When finished, ask them each to fill out a conflict resolution question sheet about their experience.

HOMEWORK: Write about a conflict you are having right now with someone. What can you do to try to resolve the conflict? Is it realistic to try to resolve the conflict now? Please explain.

CONFLICT RESOLUTION ROLE-PLAYS

DIRECTIONS: Choose one of the situations below and act out a solution to the conflict. When finished, fill out the conflict resolution form you will get from your teacher.

You and a friend are applying for the same part-time job. There is only one position at the store. Your friend told you to back off because he wants the job.

Your boyfriend/girlfriend has been spending quite a bit of time with your best friend. You think they are becoming more than just friends.

Your English teacher accuses you of cheating on a test. You have defended your position because you did not cheat, but you ended up yelling at your teacher.

A friend is supposed to meet you for tutoring every Monday at the same time. She is late every Monday and has some lame excuse. You told her that you wouldn't tutor her anymore if she continues to be irresponsible.

Your sister has borrowed some money from you and has not paid it back. She tells you that she will pay you back next week, but you need money to go on a school trip tomorrow.

CONFLICT RESOLUTION QUESTIONS

DIRECTIONS: Answer each of the following questions based on today's role-playing activity.

1. Did you feel that your partner used good communication skills during the role-play? If so, which skills were used?

   _____

   _____

2. Were either of you passive or aggressive during the role-play? If so, which was it and how did you know?

   _____

   _____

3. Did you both have your emotions under control?

   _____

   _____

4. What was the source of your conflict?

   _____

   _____

GOOD CHARACTER

5. How many possible solutions did you come up with?

_____

_____

6. At any time did you feel like you needed a mediator? When?

_____

_____

7. Which values did your partner show during the role-play?

_____

_____

8. What was the final decision? What was the solution to your conflict?

_____

_____

9. Are you happy with the outcome? Please explain.

_____

_____

LESSON 69: RECOGNIZING PROBLEMS
UNIT: CONFLICT RESOLUTION AND PROBLEM SOLVING

OBJECTIVE: To help students recognize a true problem and understand how and why we create problems for ourselves.

Group Activity:

1. Define a problem as anything that bothers you, is a source of personal trouble, or causes stress.

2. Discuss the three areas that are the cause of problems.
   - Our feelings
   - Our behaviors
   - Our attitudes

   Talk about how the above categories can coincide with the four basic psychological needs (relationship, capability, independence, pleasure).

3. Ask how we can be the cause of our own problems. Examples: by the way we think, by the way we feel, by our lack of self-control, etc.

ACTIVITY: Complete "Is this a Problem?" activity on the next page and discuss the results when finished.

HOMEWORK: Write about a problem you are currently having. Is it a real problem or is it a situation that has been exaggerated by your thinking or low self-esteem?

IS THIS A PROBLEM?

DIRECTIONS: Read each of the situations below and decide if it is a problem that needs to be solved or if it is something else. On the line either write problem or explain why it is not.

1. Jayne's boyfriend has been spending less and less time with her. She is starting to get suspicious.

   _____

2. You and a friend frequently use each other's lockers. A teacher walking by knows that this is not your locker and writes you up.

   _____

3. You are worried about your father who is in the hospital.

   _____

4. You criticize a friend for being late to meet you and now the two of you are not speaking.

   _____

5. You have been in a serious relationship for a year and your partner is asking you to do things you are not ready for, but you are afraid of a break-up.

   _____

6. The coach benches you for not participating in a drill. You yell at him, "You're a lousy coach and I don't want to play anyway!"

   _____

7. You are browsing through a rack of clothes and see a shirt you like, but you don't have any money. Maybe no one will see you take it.

   _____

8. A classmate continues to ask you for your homework so he can copy it. Even though you keep saying no, he still bothers you.

   _____

9. At the suggestion of your mother, you joined the swim team, but secretly you are afraid of the water. You don't want to disappoint her.

   _____

LESSON 70: PROBLEM SOLVING
UNIT: CONFLICT RESOLUTION AND PROBLEM SOLVING

OBJECTIVE:

To understand the necessary steps to take when trying to solve a problem.

Group Activity:

Discuss the steps used to solve problems.

- *Describe the problem.* Be as detailed as possible.

- *Brainstorm things you can do about the situation.* No matter how foolish an idea may be, write it down.

- *Think about the consequences—what might happen.* Based on the above list, write what will happen for each thing on the list. (If I do _____, _____ will happen.)

- *Choose the best option and create a plan.* Outline a step-by-step plan.

- *Act on the plan and if it fails, try another option.* Go to the next best option on the list.

ACTIVITY:

Divide the class into small groups and ask them to think about a problem either in school or at home. Each group solves the problem together using the above steps and reports on the results when finished.

HOMEWORK:

Try to solve a problem you are having with a friend. Use the steps discussed in class today.

LESSON 71: PROBLEM-SOLVING APPLICATION
UNIT: CONFLICT RESOLUTION AND PROBLEM SOLVING

OBJECTIVE: To allow students to practice their problem-solving skills and to help them recognize how they are showing their values when they use problem-solving skills.

Group Activity:

1. Review the steps to problem solving.

2. Discuss how we can struggle the most with our inner problems. These are usually moral issues where we must decide right from wrong. Sample moral issues:

   • Should you report a student you know is cheating?

   • Should you stand up for someone who is being teased, even though it isn't cool?

ACTIVITY: Distribute an index card to each student. On the index card, the student must write about a problem (not necessarily his/her own problem). Collect the cards and redistribute. Students solve the problem on the card using the sheet on the next page.

HOMEWORK: What do think is hard about trying to solve problems? What are some of the things that get in the way of finding a solution? Please explain.

PROBLEM-SOLVING WORKSHEET

DIRECTIONS: Use the worksheet below to solve the problem given to you. Be sure your brainstorm list includes at least 3 things you can do about the situation.

DESCRIBE THE PROBLEM (In detail)

BRAINSTORM THINGS TO DO

1.

2.

3.

THINK ABOUT THE CONSEQUENCES (If I do #1, this will happen)

1.

2.

3.

CHOOSE THE BEST OPTION (Please explain why)

CONFLICT RESOLUTION & PROBLEM-SOLVING

QUOTATIONS OF THE WEEK

"The answer is contained within the question, and in the state of the problem lies the solution."

- Frank Siccone-

"A problem well stated is half solved."

- John Dewey -

"You cannot shake hands with a clenched fist."

- Indira Gandhi -

"Upon the heat and flame of thy distemper, sprinkle cool patience."

- Queen Gertrude in
Shakespeare's Hamlet -

Teacher tip:

Pin one of the quotations to a bulletin board and ask students to reflect on what is said, apply it to their thinking, and explain if they agree with it. You may have them write about it in their value journals.

DECISION MAKING AND GOAL SETTING

Many people have difficulty making decisions. This unit will provide lessons to help students understand the complexities of making a calculated decision, how to weigh the pros and cons, and how to muster the courage to take a risk when necessary. They will also understand that it is not always necessary to take a risk when making a decision. Students learn to explore all their options and how to overcome obstacles that get in the way of achieving what they set out to do. Students learn the difference between realistic and unrealistic goals, how to set goals, and why it is important to keep the commitments they have made. These lessons emphasize good character in making decisions and setting goals as well as taking responsibility and avoiding excuses.

LESSON 72: MAKING A GOOD DECISION
UNIT: DECISION MAKING AND GOAL SETTING

OBJECTIVE: To learn the steps necessary for making a well-thought-out decision, including weighing the pros and cons.

Group Activity:

1. Discuss what is necessary to make a good, informed decision. Go through the steps below and answer any necessary questions.

   - State the problem or choice that must be made.
   - Outline what you know about the situation already.
   - Gather more information if necessary.
   - Make a pro and con list for each choice and consequences.
   - Choose what to do.

2. Practice these steps with the following situation together as a class:

   The big school dance is this Friday and two people asked you to go. You like things about both of them. Decide who to go to the dance with.

ACTIVITY: In-class journal: Write about a big decision you have to make. Explain why you must make this decision and outline how you will make your choice.

HOMEWORK: Write about the biggest decision you've ever had to make. How did you come to your decision? Was it the right one?

LESSON 73: WEIGHING THE PROS AND CONS
UNIT: DECISION MAKING AND GOAL SETTING

OBJECTIVE: To understand the importance of weighing the pros and cons when making a calculated decision.

Group Activity:

Discuss what it means to weigh pros and cons. Be sure to define it as figuring out the good and bad reasons for the choice we must make.

ACTIVITY: Distribute a copy of "Difficult Decisions" to each student. Ask them to pick one difficult decision and write it on the top of the paper. Then, ask them to fold the paper in half vertically and construct a pro and con list for their decision.

HOMEWORK: For the difficult decision that you made a pro and con list for, go through the steps and make the decision. Has that situation ever happened to you? Please explain.

DIFFICULT DECISIONS

DIRECTIONS: Choose one of the situations below and write a pro and con list to help you make the decision.

Two friends are out shopping and one friend steals a small computer game from the store. Should you turn in your friend or act like you didn't know it happened?

Your parents are getting a divorce. You are still under 18 and you must decide who to live with.

There is a big party at a friend's house. It is getting late and you need a ride home. You can't be late getting home or you will be grounded. The person you came to the party with has been drinking. Should you go with that person or try to find another way home?

You are a vegetarian and you've been invited to dinner at the house of the person you are dating. They are having roast beef for dinner. You want to make a good impression, but just the sight of meat makes you sick. What do you do?

Your family is Jewish and you like someone who is Catholic. Your parents have always told you to date only other Jewish people. The person you like asks you out on a date. Do you go and deceive your parents?

LESSON 74: TAKING RISKS
UNIT: DECISION MAKING AND GOAL SETTING

OBJECTIVE: To understand what a risk is and why it is sometimes necessary to take risks when making a decision.

Group Activity:

1. Define a *risk* as having a sense of fear or danger, but taking a chance that everything will turn out okay.

2. Brainstorm risks that people take. Discuss that people take risks everyday and that risks do not necessarily have to be life-threatening.

   • Ask yourself: What is the worst thing that could happen?

   • Prepare for the worst.

3. Discuss how even when we take risks, we must think of the pros and cons. (What will you give up vs. what you may gain.) Learn how to overcome your fears!

ACTIVITY: Complete "Risky Business" activity on the next page. Students decide if the situations are a risk that should be taken. Discuss results when finished.

HOMEWORK: Write about a risk that you have taken and why it was an important decision for you to make. Explain.

RISKY BUSINESS

GOOD CHARACTER

DIRECTIONS: Read each of the situations below. Decide if it is something where a risk should be taken. If not, write NO RISK and explain why. If yes, explain why the risk should be taken.

1. You like the person your best friend is dating. They have been fighting. Should you move in to comfort him/her?

   _____

   _____

2. On a camping trip one summer, you almost drown in the lake. You've been invited to a pool party and don't want to look stupid by not going swimming. Do you swim or not?

   _____

   _____

3. You bombed out on your final exam in math. The teacher is allowing you to re- take the test and she will average the two grades. This could make your score even lower if you fail again. Do you take the test?

   _____

   _____

4. You've been upset with your partner's behavior lately. When you try to talk about it, you feel like you're being blown off. Do you try to talk again or let it all go and forget about it - maybe things will get better?

   _____

   _____

5. It's the last of the ninth inning and you are up. Your hit

could win the game, but the coach is telling you to bunt. Do you try to hit the runner in or do as the coach wishes?

_____

_____

6. All your friends say you have a beautiful singing voice. Do you enter the school talent contest?

_____

_____

7. Your parents keep fighting and you are worried about what might happen. Do you get involved and try to talk to them about it?

_____

_____

8. You have the opportunity to live in France next year, but you don't know any- one in France. Do you go to France?

_____

_____

LESSON 75: OVERCOMING OBSTACLES
UNIT: DECISION MAKING AND GOAL SETTING

OBJECTIVE: To understand and recognize obstacles that may be in the way of good judgment and decision making.

Group Activity:

1. Define *obstacles* as things that get in the way of what we want to do or the goals we want to reach.

2. Discuss how obstacles are not always negative and can sometimes give us strength. Sometimes they make us work harder and help build confidence. Emphasize that we need to maintain control in order to overcome obstacles.

ACTIVITY: Divide the class into groups and distribute "Breaking Through Barriers" sheet. Ask groups to choose one situation and identify the obstacles that may be associated with their situation. After that list is done, ask them how each obstacle may give someone strength.

HOMEWORK: Write about a situation where you had to overcome some obstacles. Please explain the situation and how you overcame the obstacles.

BREAKING THROUGH BARRIERS

DIRECTIONS: Choose one of the situations below and brainstorm the obstacles that must be overcome in order to give us strength.

The captain of the basketball team got into a car accident and broke his leg just before the playoffs.

An African-American woman is going for the same job as a Caucasian man. She is much more qualified than he is. How can she earn the job?

You walked in on your best friend changing his grade in the teacher's plan book. He begs you not to tell anyone. What do you do?

Jim and Nancy have been dating for two years and he breaks up with her to go out with someone else. What can Nancy do to cope?

You want to go to college, but don't have the confidence because everyone has always told you that you don't have the ability to do college work.

You really want to run for student government but you don't have very good public speaking skills. In fact, standing in front of a crowd makes you feel nauseated.

LESSON 76: REALISTIC AND UNREALISTIC GOALS
UNIT: DECISION MAKING AND GOAL SETTING

OBJECTIVE: To help students understand the difference between realistic and unrealistic goals.

Group Activity:

1. Discuss the differences between realistic and unrealistic goals. Explain that we may want something, but there may be reasons why we cannot have or do something we would like.

2. Ask students to make a wish list of things they want to achieve in their lives. You may want to break this down into smaller increments (i.e., 5 or 10 years).

3. Ask students to go through lists and place a U for unrealistic or an R for realistic by each item. Discuss results when finished.

ACTIVITY: Complete "Too Good To Be True?" activity on the next page. Discuss results when finished.

HOMEWORK: Based on the questionnaire above, how do you think you should change your goals? Please explain.

TOO GOOD TO BE TRUE?

DIRECTIONS: Complete the following questionnaire to see how realistic you are about your goals.

Y = yes, this is true.
N = no, this is not true.
S = sometimes I feel this way.

_____ 1. I think I can do anything I put my mind to.

_____ 2. I am usually calm and cool, even under pressure.

_____ 3. Even if I was told I couldn't do something, I would do it anyway.

_____ 4. I usually take advice when it is given to me.

_____ 5. I disagree with advice when it is given to me, but I try to listen.

_____ 6. I know I will go on to college someday.

_____ 7. If I fail at something, I usually give up.

_____ 8. I am a procrastinator and have trouble sticking to time schedules.

_____ 9. I believe that I will be famous, no one has noticed me yet.

_____ 10. I would rather have little successes than experience big success all at once.

_____ 11. I wonder why things happen to other people and not me.

_____ 12. I am outgoing and have no trouble meeting people.

_____ 13. I get frustrated easily.

LESSON 77: SETTING REALISTIC GOALS
UNIT: DECISION MAKING AND GOAL SETTING

OBJECTIVE: To help students follow the steps necessary to set realistic and achievable goals.

Group Activity:

1. Outline and discuss the steps that we should take to set goals and increase our chances for success.

    - Define what it is you want to achieve. What do you want to do? Be specific!

    - Set up a list of things you *can* do. (Checklists work well.)

    - Develop a plan of action. What are your abilities?

    - Develop a time table so that you do one thing in a specific amount of time. (Small successes help achieve goals.)

    - Take action on your goal and be responsible. You will face frustration, but don't give up!

ACTIVITY: Divide the class into small groups. Give each of them an index card with a general goal on it. (I want to lose weight, I want to be successful, etc.) Ask the groups to use the above steps and create a plan of action for these goals.

HOMEWORK: Write about a realistic goal you would like to achieve.

LESSON 78: SHORT-TERM & LONG-TERM GOALS
UNIT: DECISION MAKING AND GOAL SETTING

OBJECTIVE: To understand the difference between long-term and short-term goals, as well as how short-term goals can develop into long-term goals.

Group Activity:

1. Define *long-term* and *short-term goals* and brainstorm examples of each.

   • *Long-term:* A goal you would like to achieve in 10 years or during your lifetime. (Go to college, travel around Europe, etc.)

   • *Short-term:* A goal you would like to achieve within a month, weeks, a year or two, etc. (Lose 10 lbs., get better grades, etc.)

2. Discuss how short-term goals can help achieve long-term goals by providing the feeling of success and confidence needed to strive for final results.

ACTIVITY: Complete "Long or Short?" activity on the next page and discuss the results when finished.

HOMEWORK: Write about one long-term and one short-term goal you would like to achieve.

LONG OR SHORT?

GOOD CHARACTER

DIRECTIONS: Read each of the goals below and decide if it is a long-term or short-term goal. Write which one in the box provided.

1. You would like to get an "A" in your social studies class.

2. You would like to go out for the football team.

3. You want to go to a big university.

4. You want to stop fighting with your little brother who tags along with you whenever he can.

5. You want to ask one of the 'popular crowd' to go out with you.

6. You want to get your driver's license.

7. You want to be on the all-star basketball team.

8. You want to play the lead in the school drama production.

9. You want to buy your own car.

10. You want to spend more time with your boyfriend/girlfriend.

LESSON 79: MAKING EXCUSES
UNIT: DECISION MAKING AND GOAL SETTING

OBJECTIVE: To recognize when we are making excuses and practice taking responsibility for the decisions we make and the goals we set.

Group Activity:

1. Define *excuses* as an explanation for why we did not do something, cannot do something or have what we want.

2. Discuss how excuses take us away from achieving our goals and how making excuses temporarily allows us to not take responsibility for our actions, but that responsibility does not go away.

3. Emphasize the power of positive thinking. We can do anything we put our minds to.

ACTIVITY: Complete "Excuses, Excuses" activity on the next page and share results when finished.

HOMEWORK: For what things do you make excuses? Why do you make an excuse rather than accept responsibility?

EXCUSES, EXCUSES!

DIRECTIONS: Read each of the excuses below and correct the statement with a responsible answer to the situation.

1. I didn't get my homework done because I had other homework too.

   _____

   _____

2. I didn't make it on time because I overslept.

   _____

   _____

3. Why try to get an "A"? I'm awful at math, and when will I ever use this?

   _____

   _____

4. I would like to be popular, but I'm not cool enough.

   _____

   _____

5. I can't join the soccer team, I'm not fast and I hate to run.

   _____

   _____

6. The yearbook page wasn't done because nobody told me I had to finish it today.

_____

_____

7. I don't like to read, and the books are too boring.

_____

_____

8. I want to lose weight, but I keep eating out at fast food places. I can always start exercising—that will burn off those calories.

_____

_____

LESSON 80: HONORING COMMITMENTS
UNIT: DECISION MAKING AND GOAL SETTING

OBJECTIVE: To help students understand the importance of taking responsibility for their actions and honoring the commitments they have made.

Group Activity:

1. Define *commitment* as making a promise to do what you say you will do.

2. Brainstorm commitments that we make in our lives.

   • Finishing homework on time.

   • Helping someone when we said we would help them.

   • Not quitting when we are frustrated about reaching our goals.

3. Emphasize that we are honoring ourselves when we have the drive to finish what we have started.

ACTIVITY: Complete "Are You Committed?" questionnaire. Students answer questions to see if they honor their commitments. Discuss results when finished.

HOMEWORK: What is a recent commitment you have made that you feel that you must honor? Please explain.

ARE YOU COMMITTED?

DIRECTIONS: *Answer the questions below to see how committed you are in different situations.*

A = Always · N = Never · S = Sometimes

_____ 1. I have a hard time saying no to others who ask me to do things.

_____ 2. I like to help other people.

_____ 3. I tell people that I will do things and back out at the last minute.

_____ 4. I get frustrated when things don't go the way I planned.

_____ 5. I commit to more than one thing—I can handle it.

_____ 6. People get angry with me because I don't finish things on time.

_____ 7. I often make excuses when I don't get things done on time or I am late.

_____ 8. It is hard to finish what I have started.

_____ 9. When people criticize me, I give up. Maybe they are right.

_____ 10. I have dated more than one person at a time.

_____ 11. I feel irresponsible when I don't finish things on time.

_____ 12. I am involved in clubs and/or I do volunteer work.

DECISION MAKING
& GOAL SETTING

QUOTATIONS OF THE WEEK:

> "The difference between a successful person and others
> is not a lack of strength, not a lack of knowledge,
> but rather a lack of will."
> - Vince Lombardi -

> "Obstacles are those frightful things you see when
> you take your eyes off your goals."
> - Anonymous -

> "I am only one, but I am one. I can't do everything,
> but I can do something."
> - Unknown -

> "Often the difference between a successful man and
> a failure is... the courage one has to bet on his ideas,
> to take a calculated risk—and to act."
> - Maxwell Maltz -

> "All adventures, especially into new territory, are scary."
> - Sally Ride -

> "Do not follow where the path may lead.
> Go instead where there is no path and leave a trail."
> - Muriel Strade -

Teacher tip:

*Pin one of the quotations to a bulletin board
and ask students to reflect on what is said,
apply it to their thinking and explain if they
agree with it. You may have them write
about it in their value journals.*

ALTERNATE CLASSROOM ACTIVITIES

SOCIAL SKILL OF THE MONTH

The social skill of the month is something that can be used school-wide or in the classroom. Each month, the students choose a different social skill for everyone to follow for the entire month.

It is recommended that the social skill of the month be posted, using bright colors and large letters, so as to ensure visibility within the classroom.

Once the social skill of the month is chosen, students offer helpful hints as to how to follow the social skill. Teachers may choose to monitor behavior by making a checklist for each student and at the end of the period, asking each student if he or she has followed the social skill.

EXAMPLE: FOLLOWING DIRECTIONS

1. Stop what you are doing and make eye contact with the person who is speaking.

2. Listen to what is said without interrupting.

3. Ask questions if you do not understand.

Sample Social Skills

Refraining from Gossiping	Respecting Personal Space
Reading Body Language	Using "I" Statements
Recognizing Emotions	Making Eye Contact
Listening without Interrupting	Recognizing Stressful Situations
Asking Appropriate Questions	Handling Anger
Making Choices	Resisting Peer Pressure
Accepting Criticism	Giving Praise
Taking Responsibility	Offering Your Assistance
Overcoming Fears	Responding to Teasing
Accepting Criticism	Respecting Boundaries

ATTRIBUTE OF THE MONTH & CHARACTER CALENDAR

This activity is also student driven. Students choose an attribute for each month of the school year. Each attribute should be posted on its own separate bulletin board in bright colors.

Below the attribute of the month, pin up an erasable calendar: usually dry-erase calendars are the best to use. Students come up with something everyone can do each day to follow the month's attribute.

EXAMPLE: RESPECT

6/1: Hold the door for someone else today.

6/2: Raise your hand.

6/3: Try not to spread gossip today.

6/4: Talk to someone you normally wouldn't talk to today.

6/5: Tell the truth.

Sample Attributes

Respect	Responsibility	Honesty
Trustworthiness	Hard Work	Self-Worth
Citizenship	Caring	Patience
Tolerance	Faith	Cooperation
Commitment	Love	Kindness
Courage	Manners	Perseverance
Independence	Sharing	Humor
Wisdom	Compassion	Altruism
Justice	Integrity	Courtesy

ACKNOWLEDGMENT NOTES

The purpose behind acknowledgment notes is to have each student give his/her classmates a verbal pat on the back.

At the end of each school year, give each student slips of paper equal to the number of persons in the class. (If you have 10 students, give each student 10 slips of paper.)

Ask them to write the name of each of their classmates and the teacher on a separate slip of paper. (One piece of paper for each classmate and one for the teacher—obviously they do not write a slip for themselves.)

On each slip of paper, the students write something they admire, respect or think is good about the person whose name they have written on the slip. They do this anonymously!

When all notes are finished, the teacher collects and distributes each pile to the proper student to read.

EXAMPLE:

JAYNE THOMAS

I think Jayne is a nice person and it is good to see her smile everyday.

Once the students read how their classmates feel about them, you will see the smiles and how good they feel about themselves!

The Power of Social Skills in Character Development |Appendix

MY PERSONAL TIME CAPSULE

In the beginning of the year, each student writes a letter to him/herself describing what is happening in his/her life right now.

Things to include in the letter are:

Who their friends are

Description of their personality

Likes and dislikes

Whom they like (potential boyfriend/girlfriend)

Favorite music, clothes, movies, etc.

Anything else they would like to include

The students sign the letters and seal them in an envelope. The teacher collects them and places them in a box until the end of the year.

On the last day of class, students read their letters and see how much they and other things have changed over the course of one school year!

BIBLIOGRAPHY

Some of the activities have been adapted from other sources. They are as follows:

Canfield, Jack and Siccone, Frank, *101 Ways To Develop Student Self-Esteem and Responsibility*. Needham Heights, MA: Allyn & Bacon, 1995.

Copland, Jean B. and Nicholson, Angela M., *Searching For Yourself: A Journey to Discover Values*. Villa Maria, PA: The Center for Learning, 1992.

Doody, Mary J. and Dick, Janet M., *Fast Forward: A Self-Esteem Program*. Portland, ME: J. Weston Walch, 1990.

Edwards, Donald Louis and Yucas, Jessyca P., *Valuing Others: A Journey to Discover Values*. Villa Maria, PA: The Center for Learning, 1992.

Kramer, Patricia, *The Dynamics of Relationships*. Silver Spring, ME: Equal Partners, 1994.

Schrumpf, Fred; Crawford, Donna K. and Bodine, Richard J., *Peer Mediation: Conflict Resolution in Schools*. Champaign, IL: Research Press, 1997.

Toner, Patricia Rizzo, *Relationships and Communication Activities*. West Nyack, NY: The Center for Applied Research in Education, 1993.

Toner, Patricia Rizzo, *Stress Management and Self-Esteem Activities*. West Nyack, NY: The Center for Applied Research in Education, 1993.

Other resources:

Carter, Jane & Sugai, George, "Social Skills Curriculum Analysis" (Teaching Exceptional Children). Fall, 1989, pp. 36–39.

Lickona, Thomas, *Educating For Character*. New York, NY: Bantam Books, 1991.

Warger, Cynthia & Rutherford, Robert, "Co-Teaching to Improve Social Skills" (Preventing School Failure), Vol. 37, No. 4, pp. 21–27.

ADDITIONAL RESOURCES

The following books and videos are available from National Professional Resources, Inc.

Adderholdt, Miriam. & Goldberg, Jan. Perfectionism: *What's Bad About Being Too Good?* Minneapolis, MN: Free Spirit Publishing, 1999. $12.95

Beane, Allan L. *The Bully Free Classroom: Over 100 Tips and Strategies for Teachers K-8.* Minneapolis, MN: Free Spirit Publishing, 1999. $19.95

Beedy, Jeffrey. *Sports Plus: Developing Youth Sports Programs that Teach Positive Values.* Hamilton, MA: Project Adventure, Inc., 1997. $16.00

Begun, Ruth W. *Ready-to-Use Social Skills Lesson (4 levels: Pre K-K; 1-3; 4-6; 7-12)* West Nyack, NY: Center for Applied Research, 1995. $29.95 each

Bennett, William J. *Book of Virtues.* New York, NY: Simon & Schuster, 1996. $16.00

Bennett, William J. *Moral Compass.* New York, NY: Simon & Schuster, 1996. $16.00

Benson, Peter L., Galbraith, Judy, & Espeland, Pamela. *What Teens Need To Succeed.* Minneapolis, MN: Free Spirit Press, 1998. $14.95

Berman, Sally. *Service Learning for the Multiple Intelligences Classroom.* Arlington Heights, VA: Skylight, 1999. $34.95

Bocchino, Rob. *Emotional Literacy: To Be a Different Kind of Smart.* Thousand Oaks, CA: Corwin Press, 1999. $24.95

Boston University School of Education (Editor). *The Art of Loving Well.* Boston, MA: 1995. $19.95

Brooks, B. David & Goble, Frank. *Case for Character Education.* Northridge, CA: Studio Four Productions, 1997. $11.95

Canfield, Jack & Hansen, Mark V. Chicken *Soup for the Kid's Soul: 101 Stories of Courage, Hope & Laughter.* Deerfield Beach, FL: Health Communications, Inc., 1998. $12.95

Character Connections Monthly Newsletter. National Professional Resources (Publisher). 1999. $99.00 yearly subscription

Caroll, Jeri A. Gladhart, Marsha A. & Petersen, Dixie L. *Character Building/Literature-Based Theme.* Carthage, IL: Teaching & Learning Company, 1997. $14.95

Charney, Ruth S. *Habits of Goodness: Case Studies in the Social Curriculum.* Greenfield, MA: Northeast Foundation for Children, 1997. $18.50

Cohen, Jonathan. *Educating Minds & Hearts.* New York, NY: Teacher's College Press, 1999. $21.95

Coles, Robert. *Moral Intelligence of Children.* New York, NY: Random House, Inc., 1997. $21.00

Delisle, Jim. *Growing Good Kids.* Minneapolis, MN: Free Spirit Publishing, 1996. $21.95

DeRoche, Edward F. & Williams, Mary M. *Educating Hearts & Minds.* Thousand Oaks, CA: Corwin Press, 1998. $22.95

Dotson, Anne C., & Dotson, Karen D. *Teaching Character/Parent's Guide.* Chapel Hill, NC: Character Development Publishing, 1997. $12.00

Dotson, Anne C., & Dotson, Karen D. *Teaching Character/Teacher's Guide.* Chapel Hill, NC: Character Development Publishing, 1997. $24.95

Duvall, Lynn. *Respecting Our Differences: A Guide to Getting Along in a Changing World.* Minneapolis, MN: Free Spirit Publishing, 1994. $12.95

Eberly, Don E. *America's Character.* Lanham, MD: Madison Books, 1995. $24.95

Espeland, Pamela & Verdick, Elizabeth. *Making Every Day Count: Daily Readings for Young People on Solving Problems, Setting Goals & Feeling Good About Yourself.* Minneapolis, MN: Free Spirit Publishing, 1998. $9.95

Espeland, Pamela & Wallner, Rosemary. *Making the Most of Today: Daily Readings for Young People on Self-Awareness, Creativity & Self-Esteem.* Minneapolis, MN: Free Spirit Publishing, 1998. $9.95 Etzioni, Amit. New Golden Rule: Community & Morality. New York, NY: Basic Books, 1996. $27.50

Garbarino, James. *Lost Boys.* New York, NY: The Free Press, 1999. $25.00

Garbarino, James. *Raising Children in a Socially Toxic Environment.* San Francisco, CA: Jossey-Bass, 1995. $27.95

Girard, Kathryn & Koch, Susan J. *Conflict Resolution in the Schools: A Manual for Educators.* San Francisco, CA: Jossey-Bass, 1996. $35.00

Glasser, William. *Building A Quality School: A Matter of Responsibility* (Video). National Professional Resources, 1998. $99.00

Glasser, William. *Choice Theory.* New York, NY: Harper Collins, 1998. $23.00

Glasser, William. *The Quality School: Managing Students Without Coercion.* New York, NY: Harper Collins, 1990. $12.00

Glenn, H. Stephen, *Raising Self-Reliant Children in a Self-Indulgent World.* Orem, UT: Empowering People, 1989. $12.95

Glenn, H. Stephen. *Seven Strategies for Developing Capable Students.* Orem, UT: Empowering People, 1998. $14.95

Goleman, Daniel. Emotional Intelligence: Why It Can Matter More Than IQ. New York, NY: Bantam Books, 1995. $13.95

Goleman, Daniel. Emotional Intelligence: A New Vision For Educators (Video). National Professional Resources, 1996. $89.95

Harris, Pat, et al. *Character Education: Application in the Classroom, Secondary Edition* (Video). National Professional Resources, 1998. $89.95

Healy, Jane M. *Failure to Connect.* New York, NY: Simon & Schuster, 1998. $25.00

Heath, Douglas. *Schools of Hope: Developing Mind & Character in Today's Youth.* San Francisco, CA: Jossey-Bass, 1994. $34.95

Hillman, James. *Soul's Code.* New York, NY: Random House, 1996. $23.00

Hoffman, Judith B. & Lee, Anne R. *Character Education Workbook: For School Boards, Administrators & Community Leaders*. Chapel Hill, NC: Character Development Publishing, 1997. $12.00

Jackson, Philip W. Boostrom, Robert E., & Hansen, David T. *Moral Life of Schools*. San Francisco, CA: Jossey-Bass, 1993. $30.95

Josephson, Michael & & Hanson, Wes. *Power of Character: Prominent Americans Talk About Life, Family, Work, Values & More*. San Francisco, CA: Jossey-Bass, 1998. $23.50

Kagan, Miguel et al. *Classbuilding*. San Clemente, CA: Kagan Cooperative Learning, 1995. $25.00

Kagan, Laurie, et al. *Teambuilding*. San Clemente, CA: Kagan Cooperative Learning, 1997. $25.00

Kagan, *Spencer. Building Character Through Cooperative Learning* (Video). National Professional Resources, 1999. $99.95

Kendall, John S. & Marzano, Robert J. *Content Knowledge K-12 Standards*, Second Edition. Aurora, CO: Mid-continent Regional Educational Laboratory, Inc., 1997. $47.95

Kidder, Rushworth W. *How Good People Make Tough Choices: Resolving the Dilemmas for Ethical Living*. New York, NY: William Morrow Company, Inc. 1995. $11.00

Kilpatrick, William and Gregory, & Wolf, Suzanne M. *Books That Build Character: A Guide to Teaching Your Child Moral Values Through Stories*. New York, NY: Touchstone, 1994. $11.00

Kohn, Alfie. *Punished By Rewards*. New York, NY: Houghton Mifflin Co., 1993. $13.95

Kohn, Alfie. *What to Look for in a Classroom: And Other Essays*. San Francisco, CA: Jossey-Bass, 1998. $25.00

Krovetz, Martin L. *Fostering Resiliency: Expecting All Students to Use Their Minds and Hearts Well*. Thousand Oaks, CA: Corwin Press, 1999. $24.95

Lewis, Barbara A. *Kid's Guide to Service Projects*. Minneapolis, MN: Free Spirit Publishing, 1995. $10.95

Lewis, Barbara A. *Kid's Guide to Social Action*. Minneapolis, MN: Free Spirit Publishing, 1998. $16.95

Lewis, Barbara A. *What Do You Stand For? A Kid's Guide to Building Character*. Minneapolis, MN: Free Spirit Publishing, 1997. $18.95

Lewis, Catherine, et al. *Eleven Principles of Effective Character Education* (Video). National Professional Resources, 1997. $89.95

Lickona, Thomas et al. *Character Education: Restoring Respect & Responsibility in Our Schools* (Video). National Professional Resources, 1996. $79.95

Lickona, Thomas. *Educating for Character: How our Schools can Teach Respect & Responsibility*. New York, NY: Bantam Books, 1992. $14.95

Lickona, Thomas. *Raising Good Children*. New York, NY: Bantam Books, 1994. $13.95

Live Wire Media (Publisher). *Character Way Learning Program* (3 module set), 1995. $399.00

Lockwood, Anne T. *Character Education: Controversy & Consensus.* Thousand Oaks, CA: Corwin Press, 1997. $12.95.

Macan, Lynn, et al. *Character Education: Application in the Classroom, Elementary Edition* (Video). National Professional Resources, 1998. $89.95

The MASTER Teacher, Inc. (Publisher). *Lesson Plans for Character Education, Elementary Edition.* Manhattan, KS: 1998. $59.95

The MASTER Teacher, Inc. (Publisher). *Lesson Plans for Character Education, Secondary Edition.* Manhattan, KS: 1998. $59.95

McCourt, Lisa. *Chicken Soup for Little Souls* (7 book set). Deerfield Beach, FL: Health Communications, Inc., 1998. $99.95

McKay, Linda et al. *Service Learning: Curriculum, Standards and the Community* (Video), National Professional Resources, 1998. $99.00

Murphy, Madonna M. *Character Education in America's Blue Ribbon Schools.* Lancaster, PA: Technomic Publishing, 1997. $44.95

Nelson, Jane. *Positive Discipline.* Orem, UT: Empowering People, 1996. $11.00

Packer, Alex J. *How Rude! The Teenagers' Guide to Good Manners, Proper Behavior, and Not Grossing People Out.* Minneapolis, MN: Free Spirit Publishing, 1997. $19.95

Perlstein, Ruth & Thrall, Gloria. *Ready-to-Use Conflict Resolution Activities for Secondary Students.* West Nyack, NY: Center for Applied Research in Education, 1996. $29.95

Pert, Candace. Emotion: *Gatekeeper to Performance—The Mind/Body Connection* (Video). National Professional Resources, 1999. $99.00

Pert, Candace. *Molecules of Emotion.* New York, NY: Simon & Schuster, 1999. $14.00

Pipher, Mary. *Shelter of Each Other: Rebuilding Our Families.* New York, NY: Ballantine Books, 1997. $12.95

Pollack, William. *Real Boys.* New York, NY: Henry Holt & Co., 1999. $13.95

Renzulli, Joseph. *Developing the Gifts & Talents of ALL Students* (Video), National Professional Resources, 1999. $99.95

Rimmerman, Harlan. *Resources in Cooperative Learning.* San Clemente, CA: Kagan Cooperative Learning, 1996. $25.00

Romain, Trevor. *Cliques, Phonies, & Other Baloney.* Minneapolis, MN: Free Spirit Publishing, 1998. $9.95

Rusnak, Timothy. *Integrated Approach to Character Education.* Thousand Oaks, CA: Corwin Press, 1998. $21.95

Ryan, Devin A. & Bohlin, Karen E. *Building Character in Schools.* San Francisco, CA: Jossey-Bass, 1998. $25.00

Sadlow, Sarah. *Advisor/Advisee Character Education.* Chapel Hill, NC: Character Development Publishing, 1998. $24.95

Salovey, Peter et al. *Optimizing Intelligences: Thinking, Emotion & Creativity* (Video). National Professional Resources, 1998. $99.95

Sapon-Shevin, Mara. *Because We Can Change The World: A Practical Guide to Building Cooperative, Inclusive Classroom Communities.* Needham Heights, MA: Allyn & Bacon, 1999. $29.95

Sergiovanni, Thomas J. *Leadership for the Schoolhouse.* San Francisco, CA: Jossey-Bass, 1996. $29.95

Sergiovanni, Thomas J. *Moral Leadership: Getting to the Heart of School Improvement.* San Francisco, CA: Jossey-Bass, 1992. $34.95

Shure, Myrna B. *Raising a Thinking Child.* New York, NY: Henry Holt & Co., Inc., 1994. $12.00

Shure, Myrna B. *Raising a Thinking Pre-Teen.* New York, NY: Henry Holt & Co., Inc., 2000. $23.00

Sizer, Ted. *Crafting of America's Schools* (Video), National Professional Resources, 1997. $99.95

Soder, Roger. *Democracy, Education and the Schools.* San Francisco, CA: Jossey-Bass, 1996. $32.95

Stirling, Diane, Archibald, Georgia, McKay, Linda & Berg, Shelley. *Character Education Connections for School, Home and Community.* Port Chester, NY: National Professional Resources, 2000. $39.95

Teolis, Beth. Ready-to-Use: *Conflict Resolution Activities, Elementary Edition.* West Nyack, NY: Center for Applied Research in Education, 1998. $29.95

Urban, Hal. *Life's Greatest Lessons: 20 Things I Want My Kids to Know.* Redwood City, CA: 1992. $14.00

Vincent, Philip F. *Developing Character in Students* . Chapel Hill, NC: New View Publications, 1994. $12.95

Vincent, Philip F. *Promising Practices in Character Education:* Nine Success Stories from Across the Country, Volume II. Chapel Hill, NC: Character Development Publishing, 1999. $14.00

Vincent, Philip F. *Rules & Procedures for Character Education.* Chapel Hill, NC: Character Development Group, 1998. $14.00

Wiley, Lori Sandford. *Comprehensive Character-Building Classroom.* DeBary, FL: Longwood Communications, 1998. $19.95

Wynne, Edward & Ryan, Kevin. *Reclaiming Our Schools: Teaching Character, Academics & Discipline.* Old Tappan, NY: MacMillan Publishing Co., Inc., 1996. $31.00

ALL BOOKS & VIDEOS AVAILABLE FOR PURCHASE FROM
NATIONAL PROFESSIONAL RESOURCES
1-800-453-7461
For additional current resources, see our web site
<u>www.nprinc.com</u>

ORGANIZATIONS

Center for Ethics
University of Idaho
400 Memorial Gymnasium
Moscow, ID 83843
(208) 885-2103
www.ets.uidaho.edu/center_for_ethics
email: sstoll@uidaho.edu

The Center for Learning
21590 Center Ridge Road
Rocky River, OH 44116
(800) 767-9090
www.centerforlearning.org
email: cfl@stratos.net

Center for Multicultural Cooperation
P O Box 1385
Coarsegold, CA 93614
(800) 432-3618
www.activecitizenship.org

Center for Social & Emotional Education
300 Central Park West, Suite 112
New York, NY 10024
(212) 877-7328

Character Counts!
Josephson Institute of Ethics
4640 Admiralty Way
Suite 1001
Marina del Rey, CA 90292-6610
(310) 306-1868
www.charactercounts.org/ccwelcome.htm
email: CC@Jlethics.org

Character Education Center
P O Box 80208
Rancho Santa Margarita, CA 92688-0208
(800) 229-3455
www.ethicsusa.com
email: ethicsusa@home.com

Character Education Institute
California University of Pennsylvania
250 University Avenue
California, PA 15419-1394
(724) 938-4000
www.cup.edu/character_ed

Character Education Resources
P O Box 651
Contoocook, NH 03229
www.charactereducationinfo.org/

Character Education Resource Center
Olivet College
Olivet, MI 49076
(616) 749-6620
www.olivetnet.edu/cerc

Character Plus/Cooperating School Districts
8225 Florissant Road
St Louis, MO 63121
(314) 516-4500
www.info.csd.org

Collaborative to Advance Social and Emotional Learning (CASEL)
Department of Psychology (M/C 285)
University of Illinois at Chicago
1007 West Harrison Street
Chicago, IL 60607-7137
(312) 413-1008
www.casel.org
email: casel@uic.edu

Community of Caring
1325 G Street NW
Washington, DC 20005
(202) 393-1251
www.communityofcaring.org
email: contact@communityofcaring.org

Corporation for National Service
1201 New York Avenue, NW
Washington, DC 20525
(202) 606-5000
www.cns.gov

Developmental Studies Center
2000 Embarcadero, Suite 305
Oakland, CA 94606-5300
(510) 533-0213
www.devstu.org
email: info@devstu.org

Foundation for Individual Responsibility and Social Trust (FIRST)
2500 One Liberty Place
Philadelphia, PA 19103
(888) FIRST96 (347-7896)
www.libertynet.org/first
email: first@libertynet.org

Institute for Global Ethics
11 Main Street
P O Box 563
Camden, ME 04843
(207) 236-6658
www.globalethics.org
email: webethics@globalethics.org

Institute for the Study of Civic Values
1218 Chestnut Street, Room #702
Philadelphia, PA 19107
(215) 238-1434
www.libertynet.org/edcivic/iscvhome.html
email: edcivic@libertynet.org

International Center for Character Education
University of San Diego
Division of Continuing Education
5998 Alcala Park
San Diego, CA 92110-2492
(619) 260-5980
www.teachvalues.org
email: icce@acust.edu

International Educational Foundation
4 West 43rd Street
3rd Floor
New York, NY 10036
(212) 944-7466
www.iescharactered.org

Jefferson Center for Character Education
P O Box 1283
Monrovia, CA 91017-1283
(626) 301-0403
www.jeffersoncenter.org
email: info@jeffersoncenter.org

The Kenan Ethics Program
Duke University
Box 90432
102 West Duke Building
Durham, NC 27708
(919) 660-3033
www.kenan.ethics.duke.edu

Learning for Life
1325 West Walnut Hill Lane
P O Box 152079
Irving, TX 75015-2079
(972) 580-2000
www.learning-for-life.org

Live Wire Media
3450 Sacramento Street
San Francisco, CA 94118
(800) 359-KIDS (5437)
www.livewiremedia.com

National Professional Resources, Inc.
25 South Regent Street
Port Chester, NY 10573
(800) 453-7461
www.nprinc.com
email: info@nprinc.com

National Service-Learning Clearinghouse
University of Minnesota
Department of Work, Community & Family Education
1954 Buford Avenue, Room R-460
St. Paul, MN 55108
(800) 808-SERVe (7378)
www.nicsl.coled.umn.edu

National Society for Experiential Education
1703 North Beauregard Street
Suite 400
Alexandria, VA 22311-1714
(703) 933-0017
www.nsee.org
email: info@nsee.org

National Youth Leadership Council
1910 West Country Road B
St. Paul, MN 55113
(651) 631-3672
www.nylc.org
email: nylcinfo@nylc.org

The School for Ethical Education
1000 Lafayette Boulevard
Bridgeport, CT 06604
(203) 330-5052
www.ethicsed.org
email: ethics@wisi.com

Search Institute
700 South Third Street
Suite 210
Minneapolis, MN 55415-1138
(800) 888-7828
www.search-institute.org
email: si@search-institute.org

Texas Youth Commission Office of Prevention
4900 North Lamar Boulevard
Austin, TX 78765-4260
www.tyc.state.tx.us/prevention/40001ref.html
email: Prevention@tyc.state.tx.us